The
BAAL BOOK

A Biography of the Devil

V. REV. DR. STEPHEN DE YOUNG

ANCIENT FAITH PUBLISHING
CHESTERTON, INDIANA

Published by:
Ancient Faith Publishing
A Division of Ancient Faith Ministries
1050 Broadway, Suite 6
Chesterton, IN 46304

Cover art and design: Amber Schley Iragui

ISBN: 978-1-955890-82-3

Library of Congress Control Number: 2025940360

Contents

Out on Baal

What Should We Make of an Ancient Canaanite God?

T HIS BOOK IS A BIOGRAPHY of the Devil. In twentieth-century scholarship, the common view of the origin of the figure of the Devil or Satan is that it emerged in the Persian period. Following Judah's exile in Babylon, an alliance of Persians and Medes conquered the Neo-Babylonian Empire, producing the first Persian Empire. Cyrus the Great then allowed the exiles of Judah to return and created the province of Judea. Since much of the Old Testament was either composed or reached its current, edited form in Hebrew or Aramaic during this period, scholars concluded that any changes in Second Temple Judaism leading into the emergence of Christianity were, in whole or in part, the result of Persian influence.

Western scholars, vaguely understanding Zoroastrianism as a form of dualism, then argued that the idea of a figure opposed to Yahweh the God of Israel must be an evolution or adaptation of Persian belief in a second, evil god. However, this is not the reality of Zoroastrian self-understanding, which holds that Ahura Mazda has a complicated relationship with an entity described as his shadow.

More importantly, there is simply no evidence, Jewish or Christian, in which the Devil is seen as being equally powerful or eternal along with God. Rather, the Devil—or Satan—is always depicted in Scripture and in Second Temple Jewish and Christian traditions as a rebellious vassal of the true God.

The figure of Baal is consistently portrayed as just such a rebellious servant; he is described by his own worshipers in terms very similar to those used to describe the Devil in Jewish and Christian tradition. He is prominent throughout the Hebrew Scriptures as an adversary of God for the worship of His people. In ancient Near Eastern pagan circles, this rebellion was a revolution with Baal as its hero; it was the first in a long string of victories for which he was worshiped and glorified. But the Hebrew Scriptures consciously recast this story, turning it on its head. Baal is depicted as a failed rebel, defeated and condemned, who nonetheless continues to attempt to steal glory that rightly belongs to the Almighty God. From the Scriptures' retelling of the Baal myth, the figure of the Devil emerges from the earliest chapters of Genesis to the New Testament's descriptions of the Evil One.

Modern Archaeology and the Scriptures

THE CONTRIBUTIONS OF MODERN ARCHAEOLOGY to the understanding of the Old Testament are a mixed bag in that it's difficult to see some research as a legitimate contribution. Biblical archaeology in its earliest phase divided into "modernist" and "fundamentalist" factions, more recently described commonly as "liberal" and "conservative," respectively. In truth, both these factions proceed on modernist presuppositions and principles. This is not the place to enter into a discussion of whether archaeology properly constitutes a science or ought to be conducted by scientific means. But, when approached as a science, both groups have set out to use those

means either to prove or disprove a very literal interpretation of the
Hebrew Scriptures.

THE LIMITATIONS OF "REAL"

LITERAL ITSELF IS A SLIPPERY term. In archaeology, it refers
to the idea that what is "real" is that which can be demonstrated to
be true through the application of scientific methods to evidence.
This means that anything proposed about the past must obey the
then-current understanding of the laws of natural science and also
correspond to a kind of material reality that could be filmed or pho-
tographed. Thus the wisdom and spiritual insights of ancient people
regarding the greater meaning of events, their feelings and impressions of them, and the importance of them in the life of nations or
people groups are not "real" in this sense. For the liberal scholar, insofar as these larger considerations form the biblical narrative, Scripture is not true, or at least not historical. For the conservative scholar,
to imply that these larger considerations of meaning shape the biblical narrative outs someone as a liberal and means that they do not
believe that the narrative is true, or at least historical.

The world is not so artificial, so material, or so clockwork as these
views require. Someone either loves another person, or they do not.
There is no way to test for love. It does not leave, in most cases, conclusive archaeological evidence. Yet it is no less real. A narrative
reflecting the author's subjective views of goodness, beauty, and ethi-
cal norms does not render it ahistorical. When an ancient author sees
spirits at work in events on earth, this does not mean that the events
didn't happen. Nor is the author's understanding a claim that these
spirits would have been seen with the bodily senses at the time the
events occurred. Everyone understands this in day-to-day communi-
cations and in reading written records.

DISCOVERIES OF ANCIENT TEXTS

DESPITE ITS LIMITATIONS IN METHODOLOGY, archaeology has made incontrovertible contributions in the discovery of ancient texts. In the ancient Near East, texts were routinely written in a shared cuneiform script on clay tablets. A reed was used to make wedge-shaped impressions on wet, hand-sized lumps of clay. These small tablets then were fired in a kiln to preserve them, and the writing they contained, for posterity. Due to their durability, a huge volume of these tablets has been preserved to the present day. Most of those uncovered in the modern period have not yet been translated, and those that have are, as one might suspect, records of a very mundane nature. Just as today, receipts, bills of lading, various contracts, and agreements make up the majority of ancient writings.

Archaeologists have also recovered significant troves of texts—usually royal libraries of the kings of ancient empires or city-states. Within these libraries are texts of far greater significance. Many of the most familiar ancient Near Eastern stories, like the *Epic of Gilgamesh* and ancient accounts of the creation of the world and the Flood, parallel to those in Genesis, were found in such troves. Those texts, from Assyrian and Babylonian libraries, are primarily written in Akkadian, a Semitic language that serves as the root of most other Semitic languages, in the way that Sanskrit stands behind Indo-European languages or Latin stands behind the Romance languages. They provide valuable information about the beliefs and practices of the nations surrounding ancient Israel and Judah, as well as information concerning the history of the world in which the Old Testament Scriptures are set.

Ugarit

FOR THE SUBJECT MATTER OF this book, the most important textual find came from the discovery, beginning in 1928, of the ancient city of Ugarit. Ugarit began as a Neolithic settlement on the Mediterranean coast. It grew into a prominent city-state, serving as a port and lying along trade routes in Syria leading to Europe, the Levant, and Egypt. Through the Bronze Age, Ugarit was related in various ways to the Hittites, the Syrians, and the Egyptians in terms of trade and power relationships. During the Bronze Age collapse, circa 1185 BC, Ugarit itself fell, likely due to the Sea Peoples' migration or invasion. Unlike the Phoenicians or Egyptians, who managed to reemerge as civilizations after the collapse, or other city-states that were later rebuilt, Ugarit remained desolate in the region of Ra's Shamra until its twentieth-century rediscovery.

A WINDOW INTO CANAANITE LANGUAGE AND LITURGICAL LIFE

UGARIT'S RUINS AND HER LIBRARY of texts give us a snapshot of Levantine and Canaanite culture in the twelfth century BC. The texts found there predate most, if not all, of the texts that make up the Hebrew Scriptures.[1] They reflect the cultural identity of the Canaanites of the latter part of the Torah, the Book of Joshua, and the earliest parts of Israelite history. Various aspects of this picture are relevant to the historian, the political scientist, and the material archaeologist. For the biblical scholar, the two main important elements of these

---

1   If one accepts the Mosaic origin of the Pentateuch and the early date of the Exodus, then the Torah, or significant elements of it, would predate the finds at Ugarit. For a late dating of the Exodus, the Ugarit texts would be older than even the Torah.

texts are Ugarit's language and the picture we have received of her religious and liturgical life.

Ugaritic, as the particular language of the city of Ugarit has been dubbed, is a dialect of Old Canaanite, as is Hebrew. But unlike Hebrew, Ugaritic was written in the older, cuneiform script, while the Paleo-Hebrew alphabet is derived from the Phoenician alphabet, a later development. Nonetheless, the two languages are closely related. In written form, ancient Semitic languages, from Akkadian to Ugaritic to Hebrew to Aramaic to Syriac to even later Arabic, record consonantal sounds but not vowels and have vocabularies based on very similar sets of consonants. The vocalization—the vowels that are utilized to pronounce the words aloud—differs and separates these languages and dialects.

The discovery of Ugaritic, therefore, has been a great help in interpreting very early and obscure parts of the Hebrew Scriptures. Roughly four hundred Old Testament words occur only once, and their meaning is obscure. In the past, translators have guessed at their meaning based on context clues and words in other, sometimes much later, Semitic languages that seem similar. A great number of these are word roots found in various Ugaritic texts, giving us a much better idea of the original meanings of the words in their biblical context, although scholars argue over individual cases.

The texts found written in this language include a wide variety of religious and liturgical matter that give us a firsthand witness to the worship life of the city of Ugarit and of Canaanite cities more broadly. Chief among these texts is the Baal Cycle, an epic regarding Baal, son of El, and his various exploits and victories. Many of the ritual and liturgical texts reflect these epic stories and the way in which these stories and Baal himself, along with other gods over whom Baal presided, were worshiped. In many cases, worship in these stories involved various kinds of ritual participation.

UNDERSTANDING THE OLD TESTAMENT
TREATMENT OF BAAL WORSHIP

THESE TEXTS TELL US A great deal more than we knew previously about the Baal worshipers and prophets of Baal who appear in the Scriptures. The opposition to these figures in the Old Testament is more understandable when we know the specific beliefs and practices that are being denounced. Now that we are aware of the Baal Cycle and similar texts, we see that passages in the Hebrew Bible take scenes from the Baal Cycle and other similar stories and reshape or comment on them directly. In many cases, this new knowledge serves to validate long-held traditional interpretations of biblical texts that were previously thought to be allegorical.

The Purpose of This Book

THE PURPOSE OF THIS BOOK is to make this knowledge about Baal accessible to everyday Bible readers. Obviously, most Christians lack the time and interest to study Ugaritic or even to try to track down and understand Ugaritic texts in translation. Nevertheless, the insights and scriptural interpretation derived from this knowledge is not too difficult or strange for the average person to grasp if it isn't kept locked away in academic materials. The figure of Baal looms large in the Old and even the New Testaments of Scripture, and an understanding of Baal enriches one's understanding of the Bible.

In this book, we will survey what we know about Baal in the stories and beliefs of the nations surrounding ancient Israel and Judah. We will describe what we know about the religious practices and liturgical life of the ancient Near Eastern pagans who followed Baal. We will also work through the texts in the Old and New Testaments that make reference to, or directly oppose, various Baal traditions. Through all of this, we will see that the figure of Baal—experienced by his followers as the king of the gods—and the Devil—the prince of demons—are one and the same.

Translations and Psalm Numbering

REGARDING SCRIPTURE REFERENCES FROM THE Psalms: When the Hebrew tradition (used in most English Bibles) and the Greek tradition (on which the Orthodox Study Bible and certain other translations are based) differ from one another, the numbering from the Hebrew tradition precedes the Greek, and a slash (/) separates them.

All the translations in this book, biblical or otherwise, are my own. Part of the aim in this effort is to reveal the connections between ancient texts that interact with one another by translating them in a way that is consistent. However, this translation method and the parallels drawn between these materials do not imply equality between them. Where the Scriptures speak to a topic or figure from preexisting texts or in cultures outside of Israel, the Scriptures correct and explain these texts. To put a finer point on it, again and again, the Hebrew Scriptures take the very texts that Baal's worshipers use to claim that he is glorious and worthy of worship and invert them to show that Baal is neither. Baal and his followers may present him as a rival of Yahweh the God of Israel, but the True God, the Creator of all things, is without rival or peer.

CHAPTER ONE

Make Baal

Who Was Baal to His Worshipers?

THROUGHOUT THE PERIOD OF HISTORY described within the New Testament, the most prominent pagan deity among Israel and Judah's geopolitical neighbors was Baal. From the archaeological finds at Ugarit, we know that Baal worship was already well established among Canaanites, Syrians, and Phoenicians by the middle part of the second millennium BC. This is roughly the time of the earliest suggested dating of the Exodus from Egypt. Even when later powers arose in the Near East, such as Assyria and the Neo-Babylonian Empire, they assimilated not only Baal himself into their council of gods but elements of his worship and festal celebrations. The Greeks and Romans sought to assimilate him into the figures of Zeus and Jupiter, respectively.

As reflected in the pages of the Old Testament, the cult of Baal was the primary threat to the exclusive worship of Yahweh. Despite Yahweh's commands to the Israelite people, Baal worship entered Israel and Judah, most often syncretistically. Rather than worshiping Baal instead of Yahweh, the Israelites most commonly fell into worshiping Baal alongside Yahweh or worshiping Yahweh in ways that tried

1

to assimilate Him with Baal. Baal worship was deeply integrated into Canaanite and Syrian cultures. Baal worship's intrusions into Israel, therefore, tended to wax and wane with the cultural and political influence of those neighboring cultures.

Who Is Baal?

THE ARAMAIC WORD *BAAL* IS commonly pronounced in English transliteration as "bale." Its original pronunciation was two syllables, Ba'al (Bah-all). *Baal* is an Aramaic word that means "lord" or "master." It can also be used to mean "husband," giving a window into ancient Near Eastern family structures. The fact that Baal is a commonly used title in other contexts does not mean that it doesn't also function as a proper name, both in the Hebrew Bible and in extra-biblical texts written by his followers. Baal's father, as we will see, is named El, which is simply the word for "god."

Nonetheless, there are places in the Scriptures and in other texts where the word is used as a title or to mean "husband," and does not imply the proper name of a deity. Examples of its use to refer to a human husband include Genesis 20:3 and Exodus 21:3, 22. In many texts from Israel's neighbors, it is used as a general title, appended to the name of a deity, not necessarily implying that Baal and that other deity are the same god. In these cases, it simply means "lord so-and-so." The Old Testament reflects this usage when it refers to pagan gods generally as "the baals." In some Semitic-speaking circles, it came to be used as an honorific title before the name of respected human teachers, as in the case of the founding figure of Jewish Hassidism, the Baal Shem Tov.

Very clearly in the Hebrew Bible, Baal is often used as the proper name of a particular Canaanite and Phoenician deity. The textual finds in the city of Ugarit have further confirmed that Baal was used as a proper name by his worshipers in those regions. There is also a god worshiped in other parts of Syria named Hadad, who seems in many ways similar to the figure of Baal. Scholars have advanced evidence that, in certain times and places, these two were conflated as the same deity. Other scholars have advanced evidence that in other times and places, these two were distinguished from one another. Reasonably, Baal and Hadad likely represent parallel traditions from different regions that are not identical. Nonetheless, ancient people were just as capable of seeing the parallels and similarities as modern scholars.

FAMILY TIES

BAAL WAS PART OF A family of deities. As already mentioned, he was the son of El, whose name simply means "god" in Semitic languages. El, as the father, was the highest god over the others, though he also received or was cemented in this position based on the actions of Baal, his son. His varied depictions present him as distant, particularly from humans, and so it is not apparent that there was any particular cult associated with him in the regions that worshiped Baal.

El's wife was the goddess Asherah, who bore for him seventy sons as well as daughters. These seventy sons of El made up the council of the gods that governed the world and human affairs. Through his mighty deeds and victories in battle, Baal earned the right to preside over this council, essentially displacing his father as the de facto ruler of the world. Prominent members of the council of the gods included Astarte, a goddess associated with hunting who was frequently invoked in magical rites, and Kothar, a god associated with craftsmen and technological insight.

Asherah, Baal's mother, was frequently worshiped alongside Baal, and various myths include an incestuous relationship between the two. Such a relationship, while morally repugnant, was another way in which Baal usurped his father's rule. Shrines to Asherah, where

Baal was worshiped as well, are often referred to as centered around "poles" in English translations of the Old Testament. This is a euphemistic way of describing massive carved phalluses made of wood or stone as symbols of Baal's virility. These poles seem to have begun as naturally occurring trees that were carved and ornamented, then they progressed over time into more elaborate creations. The poles themselves came to be referred to as "Asherahs."

Baal's own marriage was also incestuous in that his consort Anath was also his sister. Anath plays a prominent role as sister and wife in the stories surrounding Baal. She was a goddess associated with both love and war. This may seem strange, as we generally understand love and war to be opposites. But in the ancient Near East, love and war were more closely associated. Both involve passion and fiery emotions. Both, in that cultural context, had the same end: conquest. Both produce a certain kind of madness. As she functions in myth and related rituals, Anath embodies these conceptions.

LORD OF THE NORTH

THE DIVINE COUNCIL OF THE sons of El convened at Mount Zaphon. *Zaphon* is simply the word for the cardinal direction, "north." This could, then, be translated anywhere it occurs as "the northern mountain." Likewise, reference to Baal as the lord or master of Zaphon could be translated as his being the lord or master of the north. Because of these associations, the compass direction north is associated with evil and its origins throughout the Scriptures.

References to Mount Zaphon, however, were not simply references to an otherworldly home or mountain of the gods. As with most locations in sacred geography, and even events in the life of Baal, it was associated with a very particular place in the material world: Jebel Aqra, a limestone mountain located near the border of modern Syria and Turkey. Formerly known as Mount Casius from its Greek

4

name, it is about twenty miles north of the site of ancient Ugarit. It is very close to where the Seleucid Greeks would later build the city of Antioch in Syria, along the Orontes River.

Much like the more familiar Mount Olympus, however, this identification should not be over-literalized. People had certainly been to, or very near, the top of the mountain and had not seen, nor expected to see, the gods standing around there. Rather, these mountain sites were the homes of ancient shrines and altars. Ancient people were aware that these were already sites of great antiquity with histories extending back into the distant, preliterate past. They also understood that shrines and altars were built in particular places for specific reasons, so these mountains were seen as points of overlap between the world of spirits and the world of men. A person could journey to these places to attempt to enter into the council of the gods.

Before the Canaanites and Syro-Phoenicians, the Hittites had used the shrine atop the mountain to worship their storm god, particularly to celebrate his victory over the sea and primordial chaos. As we will see, this Hittite story has a number of broad similarities with one act of the Baal Cycle. Thus later worshipers of Baal saw this as the place where Baal had always been, for as long as recorded human memory. Other significant shrines were located at the sites of events in the life of Baal and sites where Baal followers of the past had had spiritual encounters with the deity and his fellows.

THE SIGNIFICANCE OF THE STORM GOD

BAAL IS GENERALLY CATEGORIZED AS a storm god. This is a broad classification of ancient pagan deities with certain common factors related to rain, wind, and storms. However, modern people may be tempted to take this concept far too literally, since we have the recent concept of a "pantheon" of gods. *Pantheon* is the name of a temple in Athens that was dedicated, as the name implies, to all the gods. But by "all," the Athenians meant far more than just the twelve Olympians whom people tend to identify as the Greek gods.

In the ancient world, cities, cultures, tribes, and regions had deities. As these social units were absorbed into broader social units, such as nations or empires, their deities and religious practices likewise became part of a sort of patchwork quilt of the divine world, with those of other units likewise absorbed. The relevance, power, and authority of the specific gods waxed and waned along with the power, relevance, and influence of those small social units within the whole.

The gods of a people, then, are not like the Avengers or the Justice League. They are not a team of superhuman beings with a leader, each of them possessing specific powers and abilities. Rather, particular expressions of power and might are associated with certain concepts in the human world, and these expressions are applied to a god as part and parcel of the human worship that followers think that that god is due. Attributes that are prized by humans like power, beauty, and speed are examples of this phenomenon. This is especially true of a figure like Baal, seen as a prince and a leader among the other gods. Historically, most of the ruling gods within different ancient pagan cults have been associated with the storm.

There are several levels to this storm association. First, thunder and lightning are symbols of power, a power that humans are not able to harness or wield. In Baal stories and elsewhere, lightning is commonly referred to as fire from heaven, and ancients observed that wildfires resulted from lightning strikes. Thunder, on the other hand, echoed from the mountains into the river valleys in which many ancient people lived, and it seemed to be the expression of a booming and powerful voice coming down from the gods' mountain home.

Storms with their thunder and strong winds also rolled in from the sea. The sea embodied primordial chaos for ancient people, and the storm was able to enter into a contest with these powerful forces of chaos. This observation was important to the Phoenician worshipers of Baal, who had developed an empire not primarily of military conquest but of trade. Specifically, they mastered trade on the Mediterranean Sea and were in constant need of fair winds and freedom from destructive storms. Thus, Baal became a sought-after ally.

Seasonal storms also brought the rains that irrigated crops. Ancient civilizations, for obvious reasons, were primarily agrarian, and most people were subsistence farmers, working the land to feed their families. Failure of the rains, leading to drought and famine, didn't mean only financial difficulty; it meant death—the death of one's children, spouse, or entire family. Faced with this fate, families had few choices other than selling themselves into slavery to survive. The god whose rites promised to bring the rains in their seasons was promising life to the common people in the face of a very real risk of death. Thus, Baal worship became incredibly popular not only in its native cultures but also to neighboring groups, including ancient Israel.

Based on the coming of the rains, Baal, as storm god, was also associated with the broader cycle of the seasons and the natural cycles of the earth in general. Not only was his worship a guarantor of crop fertility but also of human and animal fertility. History, for ancient pagans, was cyclical. These natural cycles formed the pattern of their lives and their self-understanding. Baal was seen to preside over these cycles. Baal worship, then, allowed his followers to navigate the cycles of their lives successfully.

Finally, these cycles included the cycles of life and death. Spring rains brought new life to crops, plants, and trees. It introduced the season when livestock and other animals reproduced. The other end of the cycle, however, in the fall and the winter, saw the death of plants and unharvested crops. While not on a yearly cycle, animals and humans also ended the cycle of their life with death. The perceived relationship between Baal and death is complex and will be discussed later. Nevertheless, the worship of Baal staved off a winter that lasts forever such that spring never comes, so followers came to associate him with the warding off of death.

All of this background is introductory to understanding the figure of Baal. He is categorized as a storm god. He was worshiped in particular places. He was seen to possess certain relationships with other gods and goddesses of the Syro-Phoenician and Canaanite peoples. But these statements treat Baal as a concept or an idea. In the ancient world as now, however, religion is not primarily a set of concepts or ideas. Baal worship was composed of a series of stories embodied and made real for the participation of followers through ritual and other practices. We have now talked about Baal, but the stories told about him help reveal to us the spiritual entity that his followers encountered in their ritual practice.

The Baal Cycle

WHAT IS NOW CALLED THE Baal Cycle is a translation of six tablets found at Ugarit that tell a related series of stories about the exploits of the god Baal. As with every other topic, scholars have debated whether these stories are truly connected in an overall narrative. There has also been considerable debate about whether the tablets represent a collection of previously independent stories. Currently, however, there is broad agreement that, at least in the form found at Ugarit, the Baal Cycle is a single work with a coherent movement and arc from beginning to end.

The discovery of alternate copies of two of the tablets has further complicated the matter. These tablets are close enough to the set of six that they can be identified as alternate versions of the same tablets. There are, however, significant variations in the text's multiple versions found in the same libraries. The major trove of texts found at Ugarit was also found in the remains of a scribal school located between two temples, that of Baal and that of Dagan.

A scribal school located between two major temples makes eminent sense, as priesthood in the ancient Near East was primarily a matter of possessing certain skills. First and foremost, it involved being literate, an extraordinarily rare skill given the complexity of cuneiform with its hundreds of symbols. Other skills involved knowledge of rituals and the ability to read certain omens and augurs, such as the entrails of sacrificial animals. This location for the tablets also opens the real possibility that variant tablets are simply bad copies. It is also possible that the six-tablet set represents a composition that used other tablets as source material.

The complete epic cycle helpfully dates itself by including the name of the king at Ugarit when it was copied, Niqmaddu II. This means that the physical copy of the Baal Cycle that we now possess is roughly 3,400 years old. The king's name attached to the text also lends credence to the idea that it represents an official text over against the potential variations or other versions of the story that may be discovered in the future. At least for Ugarit in that era, this was the version of Baal's story that informed the life of his worshipers.

While there are three discrete acts or movements of Baal's story as a whole, the broad arc is one of Baal seizing dominion over the entirety of the cosmos. As a storm god, he already controls the skies. Through warfare, he comes to be the master of the sea and then the underworld. While Zeus, Poseidon, and Hades are brothers who collectively rule existence among the Olympians, in the Baal Cycle, Yam and Mot (who will be discussed in the following sections) are enemies Baal must overcome as he enlarges his kingdom. Baal is marked by ambition—a desire to overthrow his rivals, including his own father, and seize power.

The figure of El, Baal's father, is ephemeral. This is often the case with most high gods and divine fathers in pagan traditions. On the one hand, all the authority that Baal takes from other gods had been delegated to them from El, their father. As this authority is consolidated in Baal's hands, logically he is really taking his father's place, though that is never fully articulated as such. There is no direct battle between El and Baal. Nevertheless, El is depicted conspiring with and supporting Baal's opponents against his son's ambitions.

El is also a particularly weak, almost pathetic figure at several points in the story. He doesn't directly confront his son because he is scared of him. He caves in to the demands to build Baal a palace because Anath threatens to cave in her father's head. By the end of the Cycle, El is still around but seems mostly to be a sycophant, praising his son for all his great accomplishments and doing little else. Further, the sexual relationship between Baal and his mother, El's consort, must be read against the background of family usurpation in the ancient Near East. Sexual conquest was a means of humiliating a father and taking control of a family from him, as in the biblical cases of Ham, Reuben, and Absalom. In this case, the family is the council of the gods, the seventy sons of El.

The Baal Cycle is the story of a revolution. Ostensibly, this revolution is fought against the forces of chaos and then the forces of death and the underworld. But in actuality, Baal rebels against and conquers his father, the one who brought him into being, whom Baal ought to worship as his own god. The broad structure of this story, of a divine son overthrowing his divine father, is a commonplace of ancient myth. Whoever was the most high god at a particular time was not the original but the one who had overthrown his father and seized the throne. This, of course, opened the possibility that it might happen again.

In various times and places, as empires and cities assembled and crumbled, these shifts represented to the ancient mind similar shifts within the council of the gods. Historically and culturally, however, we now know that similar Greek, Roman, and European stories, especially insofar as they announce the ascent to power of a thunder god, are dependent on the story of Baal and its ongoing influence. In Baal we have the core, original story of the divine rebel—at least as it was told by his followers and worshipers.

Unlike the way we will see this story told in the Scriptures, Baal is here portrayed as victorious over a weak and feckless father in addition to the primordial forces of the cosmos. This victory is proclaimed despite some details of the story seeming to point in the other direction, highlighting its nature as propaganda from Baal's perspective. Baal had a gospel, a proclamation of his great victories and accomplishments, the rehearsal of which was at the core of his worship.

The War with Yam

IN HIS PURSUIT OF ABSOLUTE dominion over the world, Baal's first opponent is Yam, the sea, assisted by his son and regent Nahar, the river. There is good internal evidence that the contest between Baal and Yam was, at some point, an independent story later brought into the overall Baal Cycle. Some scholars have gone so far as to argue that the first tablet of the epic, which contains this contest, does not actually belong with the other five and is still a separate story. This view goes too far, however, as there is also significant internal evidence of this story being integrated with the others to form an overall arc.

Specifically, within the story, the contest at times identifies Yam and Nahar as a previous ruling duo who are replaced by El and Baal. This framing is a good example of a typical succession myth of the ancient Near East: The original most high god and his ruling son/regent are replaced by the next pair, who now reign. At the same time, there are scenes within the story in which El and Yam collaborate against Baal. It is hard to imagine why this would be included if this story existed and functioned independently; El would be opposing his own succession to the rank of most high god.

In these scenes with El and Yam, El is depicted as already having this rank and to be protecting it against Baal. This makes sense with the overall arc of the entire cycle, by the end of which Baal has usurped all of El's authority. The best way to make sense of this competing textual evidence is that the original, potentially much older story of Baal's defeat of Yam has been brought into a larger epic along with other stories that may themselves have functioned independently. As is always the case in such a composite work, the editor brings a new level of meaning to the composite whole by the way he joins them together.

WHO ARE YAM AND NAHAR?

YAM NOT ONLY REPRESENTS THE sea, but his name is the word for "sea"; he embodies its nature. In the contemporary world, the beach and the ocean are places of recreation where people enjoy the salt air, swimming, and boating. But in the ancient world, the sea was a far more frightening prospect. Boats of this era had to remain within sight of land and were still subject to frequent shipwreck and destruction. Even for people like the Phoenicians, whose trade empire was based on their ability to move commodities around the Mediterranean by boat, the sea was a place of danger and death.

Yam's regent Nahar, whose name means "river," represents a point of access potentially less hostile to humanity. Yam is an embodiment of primordial chaos. Rivers, however, were the source of life. The earliest human civilizations grew up around rivers that supplied potable water as well as silt through seasonal flooding that allowed the beginnings of agriculture. Although the sea was dangerous and unapproachable, the river mediated the power of water in such a way that it could be life-giving. The idea of a distant and unapproachable most high god with a regent who was the object of worship and supplication did not begin with El; Yam and Nahar fulfill these roles as well.

12

As an independent story, Yam represents the forces of chaos out of which the world was created in ancient Near Eastern understanding. While modern people view being as the opposite of nothingness and existence as opposed to nonexistence, ancient people saw the opposite of being and existence as chaos. When a building collapses, all the materials that made up that building still exist; they have just fallen into chaos, and the building, as such, no longer exists. If the structure is rebuilt, those materials are taken from their chaotic state and put back in order, and a building is created. Chaos is nothing, but it has the potential to become many things. On the other hand, everything that exists is threatened by a tendency to fall back into chaos and nonexistence.

In ancient Near Eastern myth, therefore, the gods create out of chaos; in other words, they put things in order. Genesis 1 describes the creation of the world similarly but with a key difference. In the first chapter of Genesis, God builds creation out of chaotic elements; creating the world is like a massive construction project. In ancient Near Eastern myth, however, chaos is itself embodied as a divine force opposed to the gods and to humanity. For creation to take place, these forces must be defeated in battle. German scholars have coined the term *Kaoskampf* to describe this trope within literature. It represents the struggle against the forces of chaos in the divine realm.

Yam has two dragons, Lotan and Rahav, whom he unleashes on Baal, and Baal must defeat them. *Lotan* is more commonly known by the early English transliteration "Leviathan."[1] Both Rahav and Lotan are sea serpents who live in the depths of the sea, the abyss. In the ancient Near Eastern understanding of the underworld, the depths of the sea are its deepest, darkest portion, a place of imprisonment and punishment.

---

1   Baal's defeat of Lotan is itself a trope of iconography and poetry in the Syro-Canaanite world and may at one point have represented the entire story of his triumph over chaos.

Within the story, both Yam and Baal have angels who serve them and bring messages for them, as the literal meaning of the word translated "angel" implies. These messengers should be understood to be something parallel to the angels of the Scriptures, who are spiritual beings of a lower hierarchy than the divine. While a "messenger" could be a human prophet, priest, or magical practitioner, within the narrative of the Baal Cycle these beings bring messages from Yam and Baal to each other and to other gods, not to mortal men. Baal had both empowered human followers as well as spiritual beings and lesser deities who served him as emissaries. His human priesthood and prophets mediated between Baal and mortals, while the angels dealt only with their fellow spiritual beings.

COALITION BUILDING

AN IMPORTANT PART OF BAAL'S rebellion, here and throughout the epic, is that he does not intend to be a lone wolf. In every case, he seeks to rally the other gods, his siblings, and the seventy sons of El to join with him in his insurrection against Yam and ultimately to support Baal as the new ruling power. Much like El's depiction in other parts of the Baal Cycle, the narrative presents the other gods as weak, cowardly, and ineffective, especially when compared to Baal. An important element of the narrative is a rallying speech that Baal gives to the other gods after they respond to a message from Yam by literally putting their heads between their legs. "Lift up your heads, O ye gods," Baal cries out as he attempts to bring them to his cause.

Baal receives little help from most of his fellows, yet once he has secured authority himself, they meekly fall in line beneath him as they had his predecessors. This seems directly related to the state of the Baal cult itself in the religious life of Ugarit and elsewhere. The worship of Baal had come to exercise a central place, as he could command the other gods to do his bidding. Those other gods, such as Anath and Dagan, who also had significant cults, are portrayed as having close familial relationships with Baal. Their worship was, therefore, seen not as a conflict with the worship of Baal but as pleasing to him due to the relationships between the deities.

The posited relationships between gods in general in the ancient world are most often a result of this perception of compatibility and relatedness between cults rather than a belief in literal biological relationships between non-biological beings. Even where there are dim memories of a human king who had been deified into the god of some cult, as at the birthplace shrines of Zeus, the gods who were identified as his brothers, sons, and daughters were not considered to be his deified human family. Instead, they acted as trusted allies, similar to the way close friends call each other "brother" or "sister."

The victory of Baal over chaos is a mythic representation of humanity's defeat of chaos and disorder, which produced civilization. The domestication of plants into crops and animals into livestock represents a triumph of human life over a hostile world that all too often seems aimed at humanity's destruction. Baal did not necessarily create the cosmos materially, but his followers worshiped him as the creator of the inhabited world, the world of humanity. Baal's victory against chaos attaches to him the idea of a giver of knowledge, understanding, and technology. He is a god of humans and human civilization, a god of the city of humankind.

The Enthronement of Baal and His Palace

AFTER ACHIEVING THIS VICTORY OVER El, Baal expects El to build a palace for him in celebration. This is typical within ancient Near Eastern literature; the construction of the palace for a god usually follows a military victory. The spiritual palace is seen to be identical to a significant temple in the material world where the god will then be worshiped by his followers. Functionally, for the version of the Baal Cycle that we have access to, this would be the central temple of Baal in Ugarit. A similar story would be told in Tyre, for example, about the enthronement of Baal at the temple in that city.

Cities in the ancient world were constructed around temples and shrines. This practice began with the earliest human settlements of the Neolithic era that sprung up around pilgrimage sites. The first cities of Sumer were built around ziggurats, which continued to be the case in Mesopotamian culture until the rise of Persia and even into the Persian period. Thus the command to build cities without shrines and temples in ancient Israel represented a point of tension that from a very early stage, according to the Hebrew Bible, made the Israelites prone to syncretism and idolatry. Culturally, they couldn't understand the construction of such a city.

Baal was seen as the true king of the city. The human king was his prince, his regent; this role was part of the human king's claim of divinity. The human king was the point of access to the divine for the people of the city. Baal's central shrine, generally at the highest point of the city, was the place from which Baal exercised his rule, and his human subjects brought their offerings and addressed their requests to him there. The palace that Baal expects is not just a nice house to live in as a reward for a war well fought. Rather, he expects his father, El, to build him a palace and thereby yield authority over the land and the sea to him.

El does not want to do this. Despite being ineffectual, weak, and completely distant from humanity and affairs upon the earth, El wants to retain his power and status. There is here an internal argument that worship ought not to be offered to the most high god, as he isn't listening and doesn't care. Rather, worshipers should address Baal, who had won this great victory on their behalf and now offered them seasonal rains, fertility, and protection from the destructive forces of chaos. These elements within the narrative serve as a sort of justification for Baal's seizing of power and authority from his father and creator. The claim is that he knows better how to use it. From his first appearance in the narrative of Scripture in Genesis 3, this is substantively the Devil's argument.

Ultimately, in order to get El to construct Baal's palace, Anath, Baal's sister and wife, threatens to crack her father's skull if he refuses. Anath, as the goddess of love and war, is intimately involved in the passions and vigorous life of humanity, while her father is portrayed as a bloodless, weak old man. Finally, El accedes to the demands and enlists Kothar, the craftsman god, to build a magnificent palace for Baal. The palace is built and reflects a somewhat exaggerated version of Baal's central shrine at Ugarit.

Once the palace has been built, the time comes for Baal's official enthronement. By taking his seat on the throne of his temple, he will signify that following his victories, his kingdom is now secure. He is able to rest and receive glory, honor, and offerings from a grateful humanity in his city. There is evidence from particular Baal temple sites, notably Baal-Shamin in Palmyra, Syria, that footprints, said to be Baal's, were carved into the flooring to indicate the path that the god walked into the temple to be enthroned. These footprints were used as part of a festal procession within the annual celebration of this enthronement within the shrines.

Baal is ultimately enthroned by and sits next to his father El. However, the context makes clear that this is an act of succession, not merely the appointment of a vice-regent within El's domain. This is a throne that Baal has seized and now holds within his grasp. El is enthroning him because Baal and Anath have demanded it. If, in the past, El has been ineffectual and out of touch with the goings-on in the world, now Baal has cut him out entirely, placing himself between El and his former domains. *Between*, however, implies that there will be some kind of consultation between Baal and El in the future. In reality, this will not happen. El is essentially retired by his son.

El's total eclipse is borne out by the lack of temples dedicated directly to him in the Canaanite, Syrian, and Phoenician contexts. El appears as an extremely elderly man in iconography related to Baal and the other gods designated his children. As we will see in other stories involving El directly, when a king beseeches El's favor, El instructs the petitioners to offer sacrifices to Baal to receive the requested blessings. Baal has, at this point in the narrative, defeated his great rival Yam and retired his father, assuming dominion for himself over the land and sea.

The War with Mot

EVEN AFTER BAAL'S ENTHRONEMENT AND conquest, however, there was one region of the cosmos in which he did not hold dominion: the underworld. The realm of the dead operated by its own rules and was presided over by the god Mot, whose name means simply "death." Death ultimately swallows up everything that lives, and Mot was commonly depicted as devouring and swallowing those who opposed him or sought to bargain with him. A prime example is the *Epic of Gilgamesh*, likely the most well-known story from the ancient Near East. It is, at its core, the story of a king, two-thirds divine and one-third human, desperately seeking to avoid the grasp of death and ultimately failing.

A considerable amount of debate surrounds the story of Baal's contest with Mot, both as it stands by itself and in its place in the Baal Cycle as a whole. Clarity is difficult to achieve, in part, because of the present state of the text. Clay tablets are remarkably durable, and these have survived for 3,400 years and remained mostly legible. However, around the edges, including the top and bottom of the tablets, noticeable wear and occasionally even cracking and breakage have resulted in missing lines of text. Yet modern scanning methods have been able to extract additional data, invisible to the naked eye, from worn areas of the tablets.

While all the tablets in the Baal Cycle suffer from missing lines of text, the breakage in the final tablet is at a particularly crucial moment of the story. While many sections of the other tablets can be reconstructed, at least in large part, because of poetic repetitions and parallelism, a significant missing portion of the final tablet has left behind no clues. At the point where Mot swallows Baal, the text breaks off. When the text resumes, Baal is present as an actor, and though he is in the underworld, he establishes his rule there and claims victory.

THEORIES ABOUT BAAL'S VICTORY OVER MOT

IN UGARITIC AND PHOENICIAN LITERATURE, to be swallowed by Mot is essentially a description of dying. With the lacuna in the text, several suggestions have been made as to what might have happened next. One that is popular among a certain subset of scholars is the idea that Baal does indeed die and then returns to life, possibly through the intervention of Anath or another god. This act of the Baal saga would then parallel stories of Osiris and other gods who die and rise again. Based on the number of lines missing, this death and resurrection would need to be fairly quick and perfunctory, unlike the trials and journeys undertaken by those gods and their helpers to restore them to life.

Another suggestion also relies on comparative literature. Some gods in the ancient world pass through the underworld in a cycle related to a cycle of the natural world. So, for example, the Egyptian sun god Ra descends into the underworld to do battle every night then arises victorious each morning. Persephone is separated from Demeter, the goddess of harvest, and goes to Hades for the winter months, returning in the spring. Some have suggested that story is likewise based on a connection between Baal and the spring rains that bring crop fertility.

The narrative of the Baal Cycle itself, however, contains no clear allusions to this annual cycle. The only context clues in any of the three major movements of the epic all point to autumn and the harvest in terms of the time when they are taking place. Yet even those clues are scattered and not entirely clear. Baal and Mot, in the surviving text, make a sort of wager on their contest that a Baal victory will mean seven years of fertility, while a Mot victory will produce seven years of famine. This is, obviously, incompatible with an attempt to portray a regular, annual cycle. There are connections between Baal as the god of the rains, fertility, and the overcoming of death by life, but they are not quite this on the nose. As in the first case, the amount of missing text is too perfunctory to elaborate such a connection.

Another suggested possibility is that Baal allows himself to be eaten by Mot in order to infiltrate the underworld, do battle with him there deliberately, and defeat him. Versions of this theory often borrow heavily from patristic commentary on the death and Resurrection of Christ. This is deliberate, as many of the scholars proposing this are trying to connect directly the Christian gospel to the Baal story as an evolutionary development or even an instance of plagiarism.

This proposal falls apart due to the fact that none of the surviving text expresses or implies such an interpretation of whatever transpired between Baal and Mot. Further, Christianity's understanding of Christ's death and Resurrection is aimed at describing the results and effects of Christ's overcoming of death for humanity as a whole and His faithful followers in particular. In other words, Christ conquers death in order to make a way through death to eternal life for the faithful. Death itself is defeated not only as a great victory for Christ personally, for which He receives worship and praise, but it also has a direct benefit for His people.

Baal secures no such benefits for himself or anyone else through this act of his story. Rather, this text serves to connect Baal and his rule with motifs of ancestor worship in another part of Ugarit's cult. Sheol, the netherworld, was a place of darkness and horror into which all those who died passed. There, the dead might be set upon by its denizens. They might be forgotten and waste away. At best, certain divine kings in the underworld might, through receiving sacrificial honors from the living, persist there in some kind of neutral state. However, even these kings, or their shades, preyed upon the other dwellers of the underworld—and sometimes even the living.

From the surviving text, after the missing lines, Baal does nothing to better this overall situation for humanity in general or even for those who worship him. Rather, he remains in the netherworld and establishes dominion there. Nothing in the existing text indicates that Baal rose from the dead. It is a common trope in ancient Near Eastern literature for the central figure to conclude his journey with death and the underworld. This is the case for Gilgamesh, as just one example. That this is where even mighty Baal's journey ends is entirely conceivable.

Baal as a deity, however, despite remaining in the underworld, would not be considered dead and gone. By establishing it as part of his domains, Baal asserts authority over the fate of the dead in the underworld. The ancestor worship cult can thereby be subsumed into the greater Baal cult. Offerings intended for the dead or for their sake can be—and, as Baal's priests would certainly argue, should be—directed toward Baal's temple.

As a complete whole, the Baal Cycle is an argument for Baal's religious supremacy. The text does not argue that Baal ought to be worshiped instead of other deities. Yam and Mot, for example, were not served by significant cults. Baal's epic instead seeks to narratively subsume smaller cults and aspects of worship and ritual life into the Baal cult. Over the cycle's arc, Baal stages a revolution by which he gains dominion over the sky, the earth, and the regions under the earth. He takes this authority not only from his opponents who previously held it, but ultimately from his father El. Despite Baal ending his story in the underworld with dominion over the dead, the Baal Cycle presents the entire story as one of victory. It is, to use much later terminology, a gospel of Baal.

When the Scriptures tell this story and interact with its various parts, they will not simply be saying that this story isn't true. They do not take the position that Baal and his story are elaborate, invented fictions. Nor do they simply say that the opposite is true. The Scriptures will pick up on the threads we've seen in the Baal stories themselves and pull them until his narrative unravels. The Baal Cycle isn't just a story, it's a cover story.

Other Stories of Baal

THE *EPIC OF KERET*

WHILE THE BAAL CYCLE IS Baal's story, he appears as a figure in other narrative texts as well. One of the most prominent is the *Epic of Keret* (or Kirta). This epic was found at Ugarit on three tablets and features essentially three acts. Keret is from a royal family that has been decimated by plague, violence, and disaster. He has no heir. As one of royal blood, he is part divine and a member of the council of the sons of El. He encounters El in a dream, and El directs him to go to another city and take the daughter of that city's king as his wife, who will give him heirs. Before leaving, El tells him to make significant sacrificial offerings to Baal. Keret mobilizes his army and lays siege to the city until the woman is given to him in marriage.

In the following act, it is revealed (possibly because of a missing portion of text) that in the process, he had made a vow to Asherah regarding an heir and had failed to keep it. Because of this broken vow, Keret is struck sick and very nearly dies. He is also his city's god; thus his illness causes a famine to fall upon the land at the same time. Again, Keret addresses his father, El, who creates a woman whose power of healing restores him to health.

In the final movement of the story, at least as it has survived to the present day, further trouble ensues. Keret chooses to name his youngest of eight children, a daughter, as his heir. This is an offense against the divine order, and his firstborn son, of course, is outraged. The oldest son attempts to usurp Keret's throne, and the story ends with Keret pronouncing a death curse on the son that he had so desperately sought earlier in the story.

Baal's role here as the receiver of sacrificial offerings is to grant children and ward off death. This role is paralleled in other textual discoveries of prayers and incantations to Baal at Ugarit requesting these same things. Though El, as Baal's father, technically outranks him, Baal is the pivot point of contact between the divine world and the humans in need of its favors. In addition to the way in which this story shapes the hearers' view of the world, it also interacts with actual ritual practice—which we will discuss later—to explain, justify, and encourage it.

THE STORY OF AQHAT

ANOTHER STORY FROM UGARIT IN which Baal plays a role is the story of Aqhat. A man named Daniel, an ancient Syrian folk hero, has no son and seeks Baal's aid in having one. His son Aqhat then suffers a few misfortunes at the hands of gods and humans and ends up dead. Baal reveals the events leading to his fate, allowing Aqhat's sister to seek revenge. Baal's sister and wife, Anath, is likewise heavily involved in the story, such that Daniel, Aqhat, and his sister Paghit stand parallel to El, Baal, and Anath. Here again, humans call on Baal in the face of infertility. Further, this story presents vengeance as a way of restoring justice to the order of the world.

Likely the strangest Baal story found at Ugarit thus far is a single tablet, possibly a small portion of a lost story, in which Baal creates a bull through procreation. The story is very literal in that, at Anath's urging, Baal has relations with a cow that gives birth to a bull as his son. The ritual involved will be discussed in the next chapter, but this story is related to a particular practice of ritual bestiality. This same tradition likely manifests itself as the story of the minotaur in later Greek myth. The practice is the reason for several commandments in the Torah against participating in, or forcing women to participate in, such rituals.

Religion as Ritual Participation

As we have discussed, all these stories relate directly to the ritual life of Ugarit as well as ancient Canaan and Syria more generally. It is a modern mistake to assume that these stories form, or imply, merely a series of beliefs that people held and that holding those beliefs constituted religion for them. Religion was not a system of propositional truths to be believed. Members of other cults in the region and beyond did not, for example, doubt the existence of Baal or the other related gods. Nor did worshipers devoted to Baal deny that the stories told in Moab regarding the Moabite god Chemosh or in Edom regarding the Edomite god Qos were true.

While the events described in these stories were associated with locations in the material world where rituals were performed, these events were not seen to be historical per se. These events were not understood to have happened a certain number of years prior, for example. Followers of Baal would say the stories are true, but if asked if they "really happened," they would have been confused. Ancient religion was not a matter of "faith" as it is commonly used in the modern, Protestant world.

What made these stories myths was that people could come to participate in them. By taking part in the ritual cycles underlying these stories, they would encounter the gods, goddesses, and other spiritual beings depicted therein. The rituals would serve to make the promise of these stories—of children, of crops, of rain, and of, in some sense, overcoming death—real for the worshipers. The core of ancient religion was religious practice, not belief per se.

Through ritual encounters with these spiritual beings, the worshipers were believed to become like them. The positive attributes—like power, strength, beauty, and sexual prowess—that these beings manifested would be transmitted to human worshipers. Humans were brought into communion with these demonic powers in ways that they believed would shape them as people, as families, and as communities. Bonds were forged with these spiritual powers that couldn't be broken without bloodshed.

Though pagans, these ancient people were fundamentally correct about the function of ritual. Worship does make one like the object of worship. The communion developed with spiritual beings through ritual is real communion with real entities. Saint Paul affirms this in 1 Corinthians 10:20–22. Whoever a person or a society worships, and how they worship that being, will fundamentally reshape the life of the person and the society.

Societies that worshiped gods of power, war, and virility—meaning nearly all of them in the ancient world—by and large became tyrannies that were warlike and plundering. Even those ancient cultures now seen as enlightened, like the briefly democratic Athens or the Roman Republic, enslaved and brutalized their neighbors. Things today considered obvious crimes like pederasty or bestiality were cultural and religious institutions. The vast majority of humanity, whether women, slaves, or foreigners, were not even considered human.

This is why the worship of the true God, when it came to the pagan nations through Christianity, fundamentally transformed the world. Things previously considered universal institutions of civilization became unimaginable. A way of life devoted to love, joy, and peace that had previously been unattainable became not only thinkable but doable. People who had never been acknowledged as people before were greeted as brothers and sisters.

CHAPTER TWO

Baal Out

How Was Baal Worshiped?

T HE SHAPE OF THE BAAL cult parallels the shape of ancient
Near Eastern religion as a whole. The worship of Baal assimi-
lates common themes, tropes, and practices. His temple followed,
or perhaps provided, the general pattern for ancient Canaanite and
Syrian temples. Having begun as a storm/sky god, Baal also took
on aspects related to the underworld and ancient bull worship over
time, as described in the previous chapter. These varied elements
were emphasized to greater or lesser degrees in various localizations
of Baal.

Within ancient paganism, divine beings were seen to have a multi-
plicity of local bodies. Idols served as bodies for the gods, but beyond
this stood the conceptions, manifestations, or modes of operation
of a particular god in a particular place and in relationship with particular people. A divine being was seen to have a being greater than
that of a human, who possesses a single persona or aspect. The varied,
even seemingly contradictory, descriptions of a god and his or her
interactions with different groups of worshipers were all true. All the
statements about a god were true, but none were exhaustive.

There was, therefore, no systematic theology of Baal or the "pantheon" to which he belonged. Such a thing would have been impossible if anyone in the ancient world had ever managed to come up with the idea. Thus the description in the present volume aims to be as complete as possible but actually reflects a great variety of ancient experiences and practices. Historical Baal worshipers, individually and collectively, would have held to some subset of these practices while thinking them complete. They also believed that the experiences of other groups of worshipers were complete, despite differences.

This variability later would allow Baal's traditions and worship to be assimilated into those of other deities like Zeus. The being that ancient Greeks encountered under that name was also seen to be the being who was the subject of historical encounters with the ancient Syrians. The ancient world was the site of many, many different pagan cults. That world, however, did not have a variety of religions, as none of these traditional practices contradicted those of other peoples. Here, ancient Israelite religion was the odd man out for reasons that will be explored more fully in the next chapter.

Sacrificial Rituals

INFORMATION ABOUT RITUAL PRACTICE IN the ancient Near East is scattered. In part, this is likely due to the fact that much of the textual remains from the period remain untranslated. Among the translated works are handfuls of texts from different regions, different religious cults, and different time periods. One great advantage of the finds at Ugarit is that they give a more cohesive and unified view of the ritual life of the Baal cult and the city as a whole.

The religion of Baal in Ugarit, Tyre, or Carthage was not a matter of theology or reasoned debate of philosophical or other principles. It was collective and embraced entire communities, cities, nations, and empires. It also structured the entire cultural life of the suppli-cants: It laid out monthly and annual cycles of feasts, sacrifices, and observances. This ritual life also established standards of behavior. Sexuality was a part of these rituals, which involved human life from the point of fertility to death. This ritual life bound the community together and thereby shaped that community in the image of the Baal who was worshiped.

Ugarit's annual ritual calendar was structured around the summer and winter solstices as well as the vernal and autumnal equinoxes. Between each of these four festal celebrations were two interstitial feasts celebrating divine events connected to other astrological mark-ers. Events in the heavens were seen to mirror those on earth. In ideal circumstances, this mirroring was harmonious and produced good order in the life of the city. Otherwise, a lack of harmony would pro-duce a cascade effect of famine, invasion, civil strife, and plague. The key to creating and maintaining this harmony was the correct prac-tice and participation in the ritual life of the cult.

The first building block of Ugarit's lunar calendar was the month. Each new moon, as well as each full moon, was greeted with a series of sacrificial rituals and related community feasts. The offerings were made to Baal, but animals were offered to him for the other various sons of El who dwelt with him at Zaphon as well. The feasts in the city surrounding the sacrifices were seen to be a participation in feasts celebrated on the mountain of assembly by the gods themselves. Baal as regent was the host of these feasts.

DIFFERING ROLES OF PRIEST AND KING

THE RELATIONSHIP BETWEEN PRIEST AND king in Israel's neighboring nations was very different than that prescribed for Israel itself. Modern people tend to see ancient priests in terms of the Christian priesthood and the preceding Levitical priesthood of the

Hebrew Bible. Priests in these contexts are the officiants of rites and serve as the primary celebrants of the community's ritual life. In contrast, the kings of Israel and later Christian emperors and kings were seen as having a sort of ministerial role in administering God's justice but were forbidden from performing the ritual functions of the priesthood.

Across the ancient Near East, on the other hand, the king, by whatever title, was the primary celebrant of sacrificial rituals in his city. The king was thought to be divine, at least partially, with divine and human parentage. His mortal human nature made him the lowest-ranking member of the council of the gods. Nonetheless, he was still, unlike the rest of humanity, a member of that council. His priesthood then equipped him to mediate between the gods and the people.

This role was imbued with serious responsibility. The king was to be the guarantor of harmonious existence within human society and between the humans and the gods. When ill fortune revealed some element of disharmony, it was the king's job to correct the problems before the results worsened. A king who failed to do this would not be long for the throne. The inability to solve the problem easily transitions to *being* the problem; thus kings were exiled from their cities or assassinated and replaced with new dynasties with some regularity.

The priests, as such, had as their responsibility the maintenance of knowledge. This began with literacy then extended to the copying and interpretation of sacred texts. Their knowledge of ritual procedures served as a resource for the king in performing his sacred functions. Priests would not only direct and instruct the king in performing rituals but also aid him in a sort of religious triage. Their most important duty, from the perspective of the king's rule, was to diagnose the cause of any form of unrest and to deliver a prescription for the necessary sacrifices and ritual procedures to correct the situation.

ANNUAL FESTIVALS

Two particular annual festivals directly involved the king. In one festival, the king and the rest of the royal family processed through the city to the temple. This was a formal ritual entrance that served to confirm the divine kingship of the monarch. He and his family, as rulers, were welcomed into the presence of the divine family of the gods. With harmony maintained, the residents of the city would recognize the divine authority of the king for another year.

Another annual festival involved the use of a ritual bed within the central temple complex. The king would spend the night in this bed. While the tablet containing the ritual is somewhat fragmentary, it describes the arrival of a goddess, to whom the bed belongs, to spend the night as well. The context of this ritual was directly connected to the perception that the king and his offspring had both divine and human parentage. Ritually, this would have involved a shrine prostitute rather than some sort of physical manifestation of the goddess.

Another annual feast again embodied the connection between the city's leadership and the council of the gods. As the gods were understood to live in pavilion tents atop Mount Zaphon, tents were set up on the roofs of the temple complex for the gods. Idols embodying the gods were then brought in procession to these tents to dwell there in the midst of the city for the duration of the feast. This feast was essentially an inversion of the way in which other feasts of the cycle worked. Rather than an ascent to the place of the gods through ritual feasting by celebrants who participated in the divine feast, the gods descended to enter into the festal celebrations of the people of the city.

For the official cult of the city, presided over by the king, the primary sacrificial animals were bulls and rams. Other offerings varied widely, such as sacrificial birds for farmers' and peasants' smaller offerings. When the king made mass offerings for official feasts, these included discrete animals for various gods, with Baal often receiving the lion's share. Often, Baal would receive, one at a time, seven of the animals that had been allotted to the other gods.

The raising of livestock for sacrificial purposes was an industry in itself. The meat served in these feasts likely accounted for nearly all the meat eaten by the average resident of Ugarit. The production of oil and wine for use in these rituals was also its own industry and pipeline. A number of contracts discovered at Ugarit reflect the official arrangements to provision the feasts on an ongoing basis.

In stark contrast to the ritual instructions given in the Book of Leviticus in the Torah, at Ugarit, the animals were most often killed by strangulation. There are, in the extant tablets, no instructions on what to do with the blood of the sacrificial animals. It seems likely, then, that the meat was consumed with the blood still in it, without being drained. The use of this method in the cult of Baal likely accounts for the series of commands in the Torah against the consumption of meat with blood in it and the meat of strangled animals.

HUMAN SACRIFICE

HUMAN SACRIFICE TOOK PLACE WITHIN the Baal cult. It was not, however, a regular part of the cycle of feasts and sacrifices of any of the major cities devoted to Baal. Unlike Meso-American cultures, followers of Baal did not normally take slaves for the purpose of sacrificing them to their gods. Most human sacrifice to Baal was an act in extremis. One or more humans would be sacrificed in some dire circumstance as a last-ditch measure to gain the attention of a god. Before this, priests of Baal would engage in acts of self-harm, self-mutilation, and scarification in order to gain that attention.

More common—though not as common as some later Roman reports would make it seem—was infant sacrifice. Children were sacrificed to Molech, a deity whose name essentially means "ruler." The infants were offered by burning as whole offerings. During these offerings, music would be played loudly to mask the sounds. Parents received clay masks to hide any expressions of pain from the deity being summoned.

One of the primary reasons that devotees would bring offerings of infants to Baal was to guarantee the fertility of their wives. This seems counterintuitive. Why would children, once they were born, be turned into sacrificial victims? It appears that these offerings were intended as a perverse kind of firstfruits offering—not of crops, but of children. By offering the firstborn child back to Baal, parents thought their sacrifice would guarantee that he would bless them with more. This dark ritual, they thought, would bring not only more children but fertile crops and fields. Offering up some of their children to the fire was the price to be paid for success.

While the Molech cult appears originally to have been a reality at rural shrines ancillary to Baal worship, the Molech cult in the Phoenician context was ultimately mainstreamed into the Baal cult. By the time the Phoenicians relocated the center of their trade empire from Tyre to Carthage in North Africa, child sacrifice was a central element of ritual worship. Children were regularly offered to Baal Hammon, the particular localization of Baal worshiped there. Carthage and other significant Baal shrines have attached *tophets*, places where the cremated remains of children were deposited.

Certain modern scholars have attempted to argue against the widespread testimony of the ancient world regarding infant sacrifice to Baal. Motivated by a desire to rehabilitate ancient paganism, they have simply denied the prevalence of offering children. The *tophets*, they will generally claim, are places where the cremated remains of infants who died natural deaths were deposited, albeit in quantities that seem difficult to justify. Ironically, many of these same scholars will claim that the prohibitions against these acts in the Hebrew

Scriptures, such as Exodus 13, are actually covering the secret truth that the Israelites *did* sacrifice children.

In reality, the vast majority of scholars have come back around to the fact that all of the evidence and testimony supports the offering of infants to Baal by the Phoenicians and other followers. With regard to ancient Israel, despite repeated prohibitions, the Scriptures are clear that Israelites did offer their children to Molech and Baal. The question, once again, is whether or not they were supposed to. The claim of the Scriptures is that they were not. This is not a claim that can be tested archaeologically.

The feasts and offerings that formed the cycle of the religious life of Ugarit and other cities dedicated to Baal, like Tyre and Carthage, are important markers of the character of the societies in which they took place. These rituals were not performed just anywhere but rather at very particular sacred places. These locations are the shrines or temples of Baal.

Baal's Temples

SACRED SITES TO BAAL GENERALLY can be divided into three categories. The first of these are temples. *Temple* is here defined as a permanent worship site of physical construction. Temples to Baal were generally found in cities, either because the city had the resources to build a central temple complex at its high point or because the settlement grew up around one of the other types of sacred sites, then a temple was constructed. While the size, adornment, and construction materials used to build temples varied based on what was locally available and the size and wealth of the community, by and large they followed a similar layout and plan.

Archaeologists have recovered the foundation and general floor plans of a number of ancient Baal temples, including the one at

Ugarit. Additionally, until recently, an extraordinarily important temple was well preserved at Palmyra in Syria, known as the temple of Baal-Shamin. In 2015, this site was completely destroyed by ISIS guerillas. Before this, however, the site had been photographically documented, and many precise studies were made. This temple dates to a much later era, the second century BC, but shows a remarkable consistency across time in the construction of sites dedicated to Baal.

SYRIAN TEMPLES

EARLY SYRIAN TEMPLES OF BAAL were constructed to surround large courtyards that were the site of various ritual activities, including feasts and other rites—some of a sexual nature. At the back of the site was the temple proper, containing the large central idol of Baal, which he indwelt for the purpose of interacting with supplicants. Offerings were made to Baal within that temple building while the remainder of the feast was distributed to celebrants in the outer courtyard.

The central idol was so identified with Baal as one of his bodies that the details of its depiction would constitute the Baal of a particular place. Not only the idol but the temple itself was seen as an embodiment of the god worshiped there. Baal temples typically had two large pillars made of different materials at their entrance. These are theorized to represent the jugular veins and the carotid artery, making this entrance a sort of throat entering into the temple. While anatomical knowledge was not particularly advanced in the ancient Near East, ancient people were certainly aware of significant conduits of blood on either side of the human neck. In later temples, influenced by Greek architecture, these two pillars were centrally located at the entrance but joined by a series of other pillars on the building's front facade.

SHRINES

BEFORE THE BEGINNING OF LARGER-SCALE, permanent temple construction outside of cities, Baal was worshiped primarily at shrines. These shrines were established at places of significance that were viewed as sacred, most often because of some encounter with the divine that had been experienced at a spring, tree, or grove. Shrines were located on hills and other elevated points and were frequently referred to in the Hebrew Scriptures and elsewhere as "high places."

Once one of these sites was identified and became a place of pilgrimage, it was marked off by surrounding it with a barrier to create a courtyard, and an altar would be constructed. Officiants at these sites were essentially local elders—not men who traveled to cities for education and then were assigned to a shrine. Often, the position was hereditary to a family line. These priests protected and maintained the sites in addition to celebrating sacrificial and other rituals with those who gathered there on pilgrimage or from the surrounding countryside.

At these shrines, prostitution was practiced as a means of enacting fertility both for crops and for human families. These rites took three primary forms: The first involved sexual relations between priests and the shrine prostitutes, conducted in ritual ways on certain prominent feast days of the deities. In the second, men sought a blessing of fertility—agricultural or human—through engaging in relations with one of the women or young men at the shrine. The third form of shrine prostitution consisted of group sexual behavior among pilgrims during festal periods.

These women and young men did not pursue shrine prostitution as a means of dedication to Baal or his cult. Rather, they were essentially slaves who were given or sold to the shrine, most often by their parents. The remainder of their natural life then consisted of being used sexually by devotees of Baal to ensure the fertility of their fields and wives. The priest or priests of the local shrine were responsible for the care and maintenance of these shrine prostitutes.

In addition to the sacred elements of nature at the site, small idols and votive objects devoted to Baal would be found at his shrines. If there was a central image of Baal, it would most often be carved and far less elaborate than those found in temples. Additionally, the shrine often featured a sacred pole—a depiction of a large phallus—dedicated to Asherah, the mother and consort of Baal. Though, as we have seen, Baal worship embraced many aspects of life, the overriding concern for rural shrines was the fertility of crops and families.

STANDING STONES

THE FINAL TYPE OF SHRINE sacred to Baal was composed of certain standing stones placed at the site of events described in the Baal Cycle and other stories of Baal. These stones sometimes, but not always, included inscriptions identifying the significance of their location. Often the inscriptions were added much later, even in later languages, by the successors of the original users of the site.

For the worshipers of Baal who first identified and celebrated at these sites, literacy was a rare thing, so the local elders maintained the knowledge of the significance of these high places and led the rituals surrounding them. These standing stones were the object of local pilgrimages at particular festal times of the year. There the elders serving as priests would tell the story of Baal associated with the place, and the stone would be anointed with poured-out offerings of oil and wine.

Bull Baal

BOTH BAAL AND HIS FATHER El are closely associated in the literature with bull symbolism. The symbolism of the bull of heaven represents one of the deepest layers of ancient Near Eastern religion. Many of the earliest human settlements of the Neolithic era featured bull symbolism and bull horns displayed for cultic use. The bull represented the opposite of the sea serpent. While the sea and its beasts represented primordial chaos and destruction, the bull represented power, virility, domination, and order. Within Scripture, the sea dragon Lotan is depicted as Leviathan, and the great bull is called Behemoth, an emphatic plural meaning roughly "beast of beasts."

While Baal is described battling and defeating Lotan, Gilgamesh, in his epic, is described as defeating the bull of heaven. The gods then become offended at Gilgamesh for having destroyed a symbol of their power and kingdom. This symbolic relationship leads, in Ugaritic texts, to Bull being used as a title. Frequently, texts will mention Bull El and Bull Baal, not implying some other version of those deities but emphasizing their might. The bull symbolism attached to these figures frequently leads to related gods being calves and goddesses being described as heifers.

That said, it is likely that at some early stage, Baal and his father were depicted as bulls or as bull-men, but most still-existing images of Baal depict him in the form of a man with the horns of a bull. The term *horn* is often used by itself to refer to the strength of a person or nation. Likewise, mother goddesses frequently had bovine characteristics and were described as producing great quantities of milk. A reference to the Greek goddess Hera as "cow-eyed" survives in the Homeric corpus.

As previously touched upon, stories of Baal's activity in bull form gave rise to ritual activities that grossly offend modern sensibilities, and rightly so. In addition to the brief story discussed in the last chapter, a fertility ritual described in the final act of the Baal Cycle became an annual observance among his worshipers. Baal is described as mounting a heifer in the underworld seven—even eight—times, after which she gives birth to Baal's son. This scene gave rise to acts of bestiality performed by shrine prostitutes during the annual festival as part of the guarantee of the fertility of livestock.

Not only is such activity labeled as an abomination by the Torah, whether in a ritual context or not, but it is a likely reason for God's command of the destruction of a great deal of Canaanite livestock during the conquest of Joshua. Some similar traditions and practices likely underlie the later Greek story of the Minotaur. In fact, Greek myth is full of depictions of Zeus engaging in sexual activity while in animal form. As repulsive as this is to us as modern people informed by the Christian tradition, these stories were not the subject of embarrassment or shame among ancient people; in fact, the iconography of these events is often depicted inside family homes from the ancient world.

As described by the arc of the Baal Cycle, the worship of Baal absorbed a wide range of cultic activity, symbolism, and religious tradition that originally was not necessarily connected to the storm god. This syncretism included the bull worship found stretching back into preliterate eras of human history. All of its attendant symbolism of power and prowess was absorbed into the depiction of Baal, and those who sought to embody such virility immersed themselves in the rituals of his cult.

Chthonic Baal

THE TERM CHTHONIC REFERS NOT to Lovecraftian horror but to anything associated with the underworld. Through his contest with Mot and his taking up residence in the realm of the dead, Baal absorbed for himself chthonic aspects. Certainly, as a god of rain and fertility, death was in some sense his opposite. The rain gave life to crops and to people, and fertility ensured the continuity of the human race in general and families in particular. This is quite different from the emergence of Baal as governor of the dead in the realm of the dead.

The underworld—the realm of the dead—is the place to which ancestors pass at the point of their death. Baal, as lord of the dead, then serves as a link to the departed ancestors. Several tablets found in Ugarit give a fuller picture of the ancestor cult in ancient Syria. Ancestor worship in the ancient Near East differs in significant ways from its practice in a number of East Asian contexts. In the East, departed ancestors continue to exist as spirits, and those spirits are able to interact with the present world of their descendants to grant blessings or curses as they are honored or dishonored. One could say that the departed ancestors are seen as divine spirits, albeit often low-ranking ones in the larger divine hierarchy.

THE UNDERWORLD AFTER DEATH

IN THE ANCIENT NEAR EAST, particularly in Mesopotamian, Syrian, and Canaanite religion, all of the dead faced one real destination and fate: The dead went into the underworld, described by various terms such as Sheol, "the grave," or going into the *Eretz*, "the earth." There was no concept of a heavenly reward for anyone—even for kings who, in epic poems, desperately seek to avoid death. The underworld was literally the realm of nightmares for the ancients. While divine spirits might come to them in dreams, other dreams granted them horrifying glimpses of the regions under the earth and its inhabitants. The most terrifying stories of the ancient world involve some creature of the underworld making its way aboveground to menace humanity.

At the time of death, the spirit of a human was believed to descend to this realm. For most, this terrifying experience would be brief, as their shade would be destroyed by the denizens of the underworld, or they would decay and fade away as their memory was forgotten. The shades in the grave could not save themselves, let alone affect events in a positive way for their still-living offspring. Nor were surviving loved ones left with much hope. There was very little that they could do to better the fate of the departed—never mind asking them to be a source of favors.

FEAR OF THE MIGHTY DEAD

THUS FAR, IN DISCUSSING THE Baal cult, we have focused on what might be called the positive element of pagan religion. In the case of Baal, this is the central aspect of his worship. Ritual life was aimed at binding the community together with each other and with the object of their worship. A correct relationship with Baal, they thought, would guarantee the rain in its seasons, offspring, and fertility for crops and livestock. At times, worshipers would seek special favors from Baal through additional or extraordinary sacrifice.

There is also, however, a significant negative element to pagan worship. Divine and semidivine beings represented forces opposed to humanity. Among the sons of El, for example, Resheph was a god of plague and vengeance. Thus the worship directed toward Resheph and the sacrificial offerings made to him through the Baal cult were not aimed at bringing about plagues or calling down vengeance. The reality was quite the opposite—the worship directed toward Resheph was intended to ward him off and keep him at bay. Rather than attempting to gain the attention of such gods, worshipers sought to direct that attention elsewhere.

Not only the lowly and weak went into the underworld, but also the great and powerful. Though subject to death and confined to a horrific existence in the underworld, the powerful dead remained powerful, at least among their departed fellows. However, they didn't rule hell as some kind of demonic hierarchy; rather, their relative strength allowed them to seize and devour the others. A major part of the horror that ancient people experienced at the prospect of death and the underworld was the possibility of becoming prey to these beings.

A significant group of these mighty dead for Ugarit were the Rephaim, a term that appears in Scripture. Og, king of Bashan in the region near Ugarit, is called the last of the Rephaim in Deuteronomy 3:11, and this verse includes a description of his iron bed to demonstrate his giant size. The bed described is consonant with the one used in the ritual discussed earlier for the king to spend the night with a goddess. The Rephaim are also listed throughout Genesis and Deuteronomy as one of the groups of Nephilim, the giants or tyrants. The term *Nephilim* is the biblical way of describing the deified god-kings of the ancient world in negative terms.

For the Ugaritic cult, the Rephaim were an honored line of great kings from the past. They were powerful and terrible to their adversaries. While ruthless, they fought and won the battle against chaos and death to establish the civilization that the people now enjoyed. In their death, their shades in the underworld now dominate it through a continuation of that ruthless exercise of power. For the worshipers of Ugarit, these ancient god-kings remained both gods and kings in the underworld—now all the more terrifying.

APPEASING THE REPHAIM

A MAJOR ANNUAL FESTIVAL AT Ugarit involved a series of sacrifices made to appease the shades of the Rephaim. This was done first of all to appease them on behalf of the current king. When that current king died and passed into the underworld, his ancestors, the Rephaim, would rise up to meet him. Proper sacrificial honors offered the possibility that this meeting might go well rather than disastrously. Likewise, honors offered to appease these kings might incline them to direct their attention away from the offerors at the time of their death and toward other targets.

These already ancient traditions practiced by devotees of Baal naturally led to the integration of ancestor worship into a chthonic Baal figure. If the semidivine kings who passed into the underworld maintained some kind of terrible power, though, how much more so would the god Baal if he made a similar passage? Unlike the Rephaim, Baal was never said to individually terrorize those in the grave. His rule over the underworld, however, potentially meant that he could control or at least outpower the denizens of the realm of forgetfulness.

The integration of sacrificial worship toward the rulers of the underworld into Baal worship adequately explains the final arc of the Baal Cycle for his followers. If one contests with death and ends up in the underworld, this would seem to be a defeat from most perspectives. On the other hand, if the god to whom one already supplicates takes on power over the most terrifying aspect of human existence, a Baal partisan could rightly see this as a victory. But the Hebrew Scriptures' interaction with this arc will reveal other ways in which it can be read.

Baal and Zeus

THE GREEKS FIRST ENCOUNTERED THE Semitic gods directly during the Persian Wars. They understood at this point already that those in the Near East were worshiping the same divine beings as they were, albeit under different names and in different embodiments. Herodotus, for example, at one point refers to Anath, Baal's sister and wife, as the Persian Artemis. Alexander the Great built numerous shrines and altars at significant Baal sites during his conquests. When dedicating those sites, he identified them with the Zeus of that particular place. The silver tetradrachms that Alexander minted in the Syrian region featured Alexander on the front of the coin and Baal of Tarsus on the obverse side.

This is typical of conquest in the ancient pagan world: The gods of conquered cities were integrated into the divine family of the larger, overarching political entity. The conqueror's unique cults might just add the new god. In other cases involving substantial conceptual overlap or similar worship practices, the gods were understood to be localized versions of an existing god. The identification of Zeus with Baal, as storm gods and divine kings, seems intuitive in a pagan context.

In this particular case, however, the connection runs much deeper. Hesiod is the first still-extant compiler of archaic Greek myth. His compilation is a clear undergirding layer of Indo-European religious tradition. Within Hesiod's *Theogony*, this layer is then superseded by the religious practice surrounding the Olympian gods in general and Zeus in particular. The structure of this actual and more well-known Hellenic cult shows clear signs of being derived from Syrian religion rather than merely paralleling it.

Some core words of religious significance in archaic Greek are actually derived from transliterated Semitic roots, and the Greek alphabet is derived from the Phoenician alphabet by way of Aramaic. The Greeks themselves understood their culture to have originated from Syria and Egypt, though ancient peoples are not always the most trustworthy witnesses to their own origins. The unification of Zeus and Baal in Greek Syria, then, was more of a *re*union. Though obviously these traditions had developed separately and in various locales, they grew from the same Semitic roots.

WHAT'S THE DIFFERENCE BETWEEN US?

CERTAINLY, ZEUS AND BAAL ARE both storm gods. Both have the thunderbolt as the symbol of their power and might. Both preside over a council of gods united by familial bonds. At a deeper level, however, both arrived at their present position of dominion by staging a rebellion—in particular, a rebellion against their father and creator. Zeus, like Baal, gathered his fellow gods to destroy his father and the preceding divine order. They not only, like Baal, defeated those gods of ancient primordial forces but imprisoned them in the deepest, darkest part of the underworld. In the wake of that victory, Zeus led his cohorts to further victories against the giants and chaos beasts from the sea.

The primary place of ongoing contact between the cults of Zeus and Baal was Asia Minor. The western portions, particularly the coastal regions, were deeply part of Hellenic culture. The eastern regions, though the residents were of Indo-European descent, were as deeply formed by West Semitic cultural and religious traditions. Here, the lines between Zeus and Baal were always blurred, with pilgrimages going in both directions. The majority of significant altars to Zeus were built in Asia Minor at the festal sites of his various victories. Likewise, Asian shrines to Baal were built at his festal sites.

Alexander's successors carried on the use and rededication of traditional Baal sites. The Seleucid monarchs over the East, under the influence of Greek religious traditions, institutionalized Baal worship using the titles of Zeus. Over several centuries, Eastern worshipers gradually forgot any real distinction between Baal, Zeus, and their varied rites. Rather, they saw these rites as part of a single cult celebrated in diverse ways and directed toward diverse localizations of Zeus and the other gods.

The Greeks and later the Romans co-opted the formal Baal cult as it had been practiced in the cities, and Greek terminology and identifications persisted into the Roman period. But in the countryside, outside the major Greek and Roman cities, the worship of Baal in very traditional ways persisted at high places and shrines. The native Syrians who used these shrines and continued these rustic traditions still spoke Aramaic in its various dialects. They, therefore, continued to use the much older traditional titles and rhetoric for Baal.

ROME VERSUS BAAL HAMMON

IN NORTH AFRICA, THE LATER encounter between worshipers of
Zeus or Jupiter and worshipers of Baal went an entirely different way.
Over the centuries, the locus of the power of the Phoenician trade
empire had been gradually shifting from Tyre, on the coast of the
Levant, to Carthage, their colony in North Africa. Alexander's conquest of the previously unconquerable city of Tyre made this transi-
tion permanent. This Carthaginian empire would famously run afoul
of the Romans beginning in the third century BC. As the power of
the Roman Republic continued to expand in the Western Mediterranean, it ran up against the existing power of the Phoenicians.

The Romans fought three wars against the Phoenicians, with the
second Punic War being the most famous as Hannibal, Carthage's
general, invaded Italy by land across the Alps, though he failed to
reach Rome. For years, Roman senators called for the complete anni-
hilation of Carthage and, thereby, Phoenician power. Finally, in the
middle of the second century BC, a third and final war ensued. The
Romans obliterated Carthage only to rebuild it afterward as a Roman
metropolis in western North Africa. The Semitic people of Carthage
were enslaved and removed.

The Romans showed particular disgust for the Phoenician worship of Baal Hammon, the localization of the god in Carthage. Their
critique was heavily focused on, but not limited to, the practice of
infant sacrifice. Human sacrifice, even infant sacrifice, had occurred
in the deep histories of both archaic Rome and Greece, and acts that
amounted to human sacrifice still took place in Rome in extreme sit-
uations. This history, however, was the subject of great embarrassment to the Romans in the era of the Republic. They covered up and
even denied the reality of these past observances.

Carthage, on the other hand, experienced no public shame for
their practice of infant sacrifice as a regular institution. The great

rage of the Romans against this practice seems to be generated by the Phoenicians' reminder of a humiliating, rejected past. Publicly, the Romans would not say that their worship of Jupiter and the worship of any localization of Baal were the same. In reality, they were just as aware of the continuity as the Greeks were, but that continuity horrified them. The Romans, in general, sought to resolve cognitive dissonance with brutal violence, and they responded to the Phoenicians' practices by destroying Carthage.

Significance of the Baal Cult in the Old Testament

THE UGARITIC DEPICTION OF THE Baal cult precedes the writing of the Hebrew Scriptures. Baal worship continued in the regions surrounding Israel and Judah throughout the Old Testament period in both institutionalized and popular folk forms. Understanding Baal's cult, therefore, represents one of the most important elements of the background of the Bible as a whole. In revealing Himself to a West Semitic people, the God of Israel reveals Himself in contrast to the gods of the neighboring nations, and Baal in particular.

CHAPTER THREE

Hey, Baal

Where Is Baal in the Old Testament?

THE TEXTS THAT FORM THE Hebrew Bible and the Christian Old Testament interact with the reality of Baal worship
in various ways. The historical books of the Old Testament describe
encounters with Baal worship and worshipers. Often, these encounters involve the people of Israel or Judah being drawn into practicing
the worship of Baal. The Psalms evoke tropes, imagery, and language
from the Baal cult, reappropriating it for the true God Yahweh. The
prophets speak of events, both past and future from their historical
perspective, that correct the claims made by followers of Baal.

As mentioned in the previous chapters, scholars often take these
passages as evidence that ancient Israelite worship was of a piece with
Baal worship, and the exclusive worship of Yahweh in Judah after
the exile was a much later development. What refutes this idea is the
function that the use of Baal cult material serves in these passages.
In every case, the elements of the Baal cult are neither endorsed nor
appropriated unchanged. Instead, the elements drawn from the worship of Baal are transformed and in some cases completely inverted.

The use of this material in the Scriptures is not plagiarism but polemic; it constitutes not an endorsement but rather criticism.

Is Yahweh Actually Baal?

THE FIRST QUESTION TO ANSWER is: Was Yahweh the God of Israel, as worshiped by ancient Israel and Judah, merely Baal worshiped under another name, as in Hadad or Zeus? To most Christian or Jewish readers, this may seem to be a silly question and is easily answered. Unfortunately, in academia, it is now taught as a historical fact that Yahweh was originally a Canaanite storm god, a son of El, and only much later became the God worshiped by post-exilic Judaism and Christianity. This theory predominates despite, as we will see, a complete lack of evidence for it.

OLD TESTAMENT SCHOLARSHIP
MINUS THE OLD TESTAMENT

CONTEMPORARY OLD TESTAMENT SCHOLARSHIP LARGELY arrives at its present conclusions based on its currently accepted methodology. One might assume that being an Old Testament or a Hebrew Bible scholar means that someone is a scholar of those particular texts, in the same way that a Shakespeare scholar is an expert on his plays and Elizabethan theater more generally. New Testament scholarship has largely reoriented itself in this mode over the past few decades. Old Testament scholarship, however, represents a conjectural discipline that tries to reconstruct the "actual" history of the nations of Judah and Israel in the first millennium BC.

Old Testament scholars have largely divorced themselves from the text itself. The Hebrew Bible has been sliced into increasingly small shreds dated to various levels of editorial activity across centuries. The discipline now takes for granted that the biblical texts are not accurate witnesses in any way to historical events and that the ideas expressed in Psalms, the prophets, and the wisdom literature do not accurately reflect the views of Israelites and Judahites at the time of their supposed composition. These scholars, therefore, set aside the text and proceed to reconstruct the "real" history by other means.

These other means are generally some set of principles of modern historiography. For example, a given scholar may consider all of history to be the history of class struggle. Another may see the history of religion as one of slow evolution and development toward some eventual ideal form. One of his fellows might agree about the development but then think that the ultimate result is the overcoming of religion itself. In any case, the true history of the nations of Israel and Judah is assumed to follow whatever historical patterns to which the scholar adheres. These patterns are derived from the history of other nations in the time period as well as the vast sweep of recorded world history. Israel's history is assumed to be just like the history of her neighbors; therefore, her religious life is likewise assumed to be identical.

With this approach, anything unique or new that the religion of ancient Israel contributed to history must have emerged very late and will be dated to the latest date that the scholar can justify with the available evidence. By and large, all the texts of the Hebrew Scriptures in their canonical forms are assigned a very late date, sometimes long after the exile, because they supposedly don't reflect the religious life of ancient Israel. And the way scholars know that these texts don't reflect the religious life of ancient Israel is that they were written very late. The fact that this is a circular argument is never fully addressed in any of these academic reconstructions.

These reconstructions do not make the text of the Old Testament completely useless to scholars, however. While the final, canonical form of the text is dated very late, scholars often date certain elements, pieces, and bits of text much earlier, claiming that they have been subject to much later editing. Therefore, any portion of the text that supports someone's proposed reconstruction can be pulled out and used as evidence for that person's position—even if it needs to be re-edited.

Additionally, other texts that are assumed to be late are read with suspicion. A scholar will take a biblical text that argues against their theory and state that it is a later text, a result of priestly editing that attempts to cover up the truth due to later embarrassment or change of perspective. Using this method, both texts that support and texts that argue against a given position are taken to be evidence of that position. It is difficult to imagine, then, what could possibly falsify these reconstructions. That scholars have made their positions unfalsifiable and therefore irrational is, again, never fully addressed within the discipline.

QUESTIONABLE EVIDENCE: INSCRIPTIONS

GIVEN THE METHODOLOGY OF CURRENT scholarship in general, what evidence do scholars advance to support the theory that Yahweh began as a pagan storm god who was very similar, if not identical, to Baal? In terms of direct evidence, strictly speaking, there is none. There are no extant ancient Near Eastern texts that list Yahweh among other gods in a "pantheon" or as one of the sons of El. His name does not appear in any Baal texts. Yet all these reconstructions are assumed without evidence, over against the text of the Scriptures.

The closest thing to such evidence is a pair of inscriptions found among others in Kuntillet Ajrud in the Sinai Peninsula. These inscriptions date to the late ninth or early eighth century BC. For comparison, the Northern Kingdom of Israel, referenced in one of the inscriptions, fell to the Assyrians in 722 BC; thus these inscriptions date to the height of the Northern Kingdom's power and influence. One of them refers to "Yahweh of Samaria and his Asherah," while the other refers to "Yahweh of Teman and his Ashera." Samaria was the capital of the Northern Kingdom of Israel, established by the Omride dynasty. *Teman* is the Hebrew word for the cardinal direction "south" and was used to refer to the southern part of the Arabian Peninsula as well as to a particularly influential clan among the Edomites who lived to Israel's south.

Identifying Yahweh with the city of Samaria is noncontroversial, as Yahweh was the God of the Northern Kingdom. From this simple identification, however, many scholars have assumed far more. For example, they posit that, contrary to the biblical account, this must mean that there was a temple of Yahweh in the city of Samaria. The reference to "Yahweh's Asherah" is then taken to mean that Ancient Israelites as a whole believed that Yahweh had a goddess as a wife. This is a bit of a reach. The term *Asherah*, as we have seen with the term *Baal*, had multiple meanings. It was sometimes used to refer to a specific goddess, the consort of El. It was also used to refer to any goddess in general, in the same way that we find references to Baals. This second usage is the one assumed by scholars here. However, the term was also used to refer to Asherah poles, be they sacred trees or crafted objects. The actual grammatical form of the word *Asherah* in these inscriptions follows the pattern for a reference to a sacred tree, not a goddess.

The correct framing of this evidence and its relationship to the Bible applies to a whole range of these arguments and bits of archaeological evidence that are often overinterpreted. The Hebrew Scriptures describe the actual on-the-ground religion of both Israel and Judah as being syncretistic. They testify to the fact that, particularly for most of the history of the Northern Kingdom, Yahweh worship was at war with Baal worship. Even when Yahweh was preeminently worshiped in the Northern Kingdom, He was worshiped in pagan, idolatrous ways.

The testimony of the Old Testament is not that Israel never engaged in pagan worship. Quite the opposite. The claim of the Scriptures is that they were not supposed to—that they should have known better. But this claim is not testable by archaeological evidence. Instead, the evidence found, including these inscriptions, supports what the text of the Bible says: that Israel and Judah were engaged in pagan, idolatrous worship of foreign gods. There is nothing that could be dug out of the earth in the Levant that could confirm or deny whether Israel and Judah *ought* to have done so. This is a simple category mistake, applying methodology used in one field to another one where it is inappropriate.

While the first inscription argues that at that point in history an Asherah pole was used at a shrine in Samaria, the second reference to Yahweh being "of Teman" is a bit less obvious. Many contemporary scholars have taken this reference as a piece of evidence that Yahweh was essentially identical to the god Qos, who came to be the chief deity of Edom by the time of the inscription. This misconception is a common one used by scholars in these arguments, which frequently assumes that persons leaving inscriptions or writing texts not only knew the state of affairs at the time they were writing but knew the ancient origins of the things to which they refer. Even were it true that in the early eighth century BC some sort of syncretism was taking place in Edomite territories between Yahweh and the worship of Qos, that would in no way be evidence that Yahweh worship originated in Edom with the worship of Qos.

While this inscription is weak evidence connecting Yahweh to Edom historically, there are other texts associating them from which scholars attempt to form a stronger case for Yahweh as a storm god. The earliest known usages of the name *Yahweh* outside of the Scriptures are two Egyptian inscriptions identifying Him as the God of the Shasu Bedouins. These inscriptions date to the end of the fifteenth century BC, and *Shasu* is the name by which Egyptians referred to the nomadic tribes of Syria and Palestine. The inscriptions are from the time period, roughly, of the Exodus. In context, these words would be referring to a mixture of Midianites, Edomites, and Ishmaelite groups.

These inscriptions are entirely consistent with the testimony of Scripture. The patriarchal narratives in Genesis connect all these tribal groups to Abraham, who lived several centuries before. Genesis identifies Yahweh as the God of Abraham and his seed. While the Hebrew Scriptures present many of these groups, such as the Edomites and Moabites, as practicing various forms of paganism and syncretism at a later point, this is not immediately the case. Moses is presented as spending forty years with his father-in-law, Jethro, who still served as a priest of the God of Abraham. Deuteronomy 2 presents Yahweh as the One who brought the Edomites, Moabites, Ammonites, and other Abrahamites to their lands and gave those lands to them in the same way that He was then bringing the Israelites to Canaan.

At several points the Hebrew Scriptures describe the journey of the Israelites to Canaan as a journey undertaken by Yahweh Himself, beginning with His encounter with Moses in the south and ending at the temple in Jerusalem. The Torah presents God as journeying with Israel and dwelling in the tabernacle, a tent in the middle of Israel's tents. Judges 5:4–5, for example, describes Yahweh as coming from Edom in the south. Deuteronomy 33:2 describes Him as having marched up from Mount Seir, and Habakkuk 3:3 again refers to Him as having come from Teman. In all three of these cases, Israelites are describing their historical experience of Yahweh as God, not positing the origins of Yahweh worship in the sense in which modern scholars discuss it.

ETYMOLOGICAL ARGUMENT

THE FINAL PIECE OF SUPPOSED evidence generally submitted in favor of identifying Yahweh as an Edomite storm god is etymological. It seems clear that in Hebrew, based on its form, the name *Yahweh* means "He who causes things to be." It is a name connected to God as Creator and as Redeemer who gives a new beginning. These, however, are considered by scholars to be advanced religious concepts that couldn't have emerged yet at such an early stage.

Therefore, they will point out that *Yahweh* could also be an Edomite word meaning "he blows." From this and scattered references to Yahweh as the God of Israel sending rain in its seasons, they conclude that He was a storm god. Several steps are missing from this argument, however. Even if the name *Yahweh* did possess that Edomite etymology at some point, it is far from conclusive that this would mean that He was a storm god. For example, He could be seen as the One who breathes the breath of life, giving life to the world. There really is very little behind this argument beyond assuming that since most of Israel's neighbors worshiped storm gods, Yahweh the God of Israel must have been a storm god.

Two more biblical passages are important to discuss in this context, as they are frequently referenced as passages where something relevant to the subject "slips out" in the text despite the supposed efforts of later editors. Deuteronomy 32:8–9 describes the time when the Most High God allotted the lands of the world to the nations, along with the sons of God. Verse nine then describes Israel as Yahweh's portion and allotment. Contemporary scholars take these verses in a literal way, saying that this verse is describing El allotting the nations to his seventy sons, one of whom, they say, is Yahweh, who receives Israel.

There are immediate difficulties with this interpretation, however. First, there are indeed seventy nations in the table of nations in Genesis 10, and the number seventy is often used to invoke the nations throughout the Hebrew Scriptures. However, Israel is not one of those seventy nations. It did not exist yet—not until the Exodus from Egypt. In Deuteronomy and elsewhere, Israel is seen as having been created by Yahweh from what was not a people. Within the text of

Deuteronomy itself, 4:19 states that the Israelites are not to worship the heavenly hosts, to whom Yahweh their God has allotted the seventy nations. The title Most High is ascribed to Yahweh over and over again in the Hebrew Scriptures. The argument that these are two separate deities in Deuteronomy 32:8, but not in Deuteronomy 4 and elsewhere, seems like special pleading.

Finally, scholars frequently point to Hosea 2:16, in which God says to sinful Israel that on the day of redemption, "You will call Me 'my man' and no longer call me 'my Baal.'" They cite this text to argue that the same deity worshiped in Israel at one point as Baal was later worshiped as Yahweh. This interpretation, of course, makes no sense in context. Hosea is not making any claims as to the history of worship in Israel over the centuries. The Book of Hosea as a whole has as a motif God as the faithful husband to Israel, His unfaithful wife. The words translated here literally as "my man" and "my Baal" are actually two different words for "husband." The first is a more congenial term—the man who belongs to a woman in the way that the woman belongs to the man. The second carries with it the connotation of the husband as a lord or master who makes demands. This text describes, in terms of a marriage, a promised transformation of the relationship between God and Israel in the direction of mutual love.

Thus, while it is stated as a simple fact in books and documentaries that Yahweh the God of Israel was formerly a member of a pantheon of Canaanite gods and a storm god à la Baal, there is simply no actual evidence. It is a conclusion arrived at for ideological reasons that then goes in search of evidence, trying to find texts or inscriptions that might, if read from a certain perspective, confirm that conclusion. The same scholars who advance these theories reject the historicity of any number of elements of the Old Testament's witness, such as the Exodus, based on a "lack of evidence." They criticize Christian archaeologists and scholars for looking for evidence to justify their religious beliefs. The reality is that they are the ones guilty of these errors.

Baal Peor

THE FIRST ENCOUNTER BETWEEN THE Israelites and Baal worship took place at Peor in Moabite territory as they drew near to the land of Canaan. The city of Peor had its own localization of Baal—the Baal of Peor or simply Baal–Peor. As was common with these localizations, this meant that Baal, as worshiped at Peor, had certain peculiar characteristics in his iconography. Worshipers also likely celebrated particular local traditional feasts related to Baal—residues of the local people's worship of a spirit that preceded their contact with other mainstream worshipers of Baal. Once the Baal cult proper, as celebrated by neighboring groups, predominated at Peor, it simply absorbed that local cult and identified the spirit or god being worshiped there as Baal.

Though we don't have direct archaeological evidence—and none would be expected—there is enough in the biblical descriptions of related events to conclude that the worship of Baal at Peor was fairly typical. As with most villages, towns, and small cities, the worship was conducted at a nearby high place, on a hill or promontory. Central to this open-air shrine would be a carved representation of Baal, from wood or stone, and sacrificial offerings would be made before him. Areas with low tables would be designated for feasting, and participants would eat while reclining on the ground. In addition to the sacrificial offerings being eaten, the tables would include other food items.

SHRINE PROSTITUTION

AT PEOR A RETINUE OF shrine prostitutes was attached to the high places. These were primarily female slaves owned by the local priests or elders who celebrated the rites at the shrine. Though such groups of slaves often also included young boys, all the enslaved people mentioned in the biblical text are women. As the feasting drew to a close, and after a considerable amount of alcohol was consumed, the revelries would escalate when these shrine prostitutes came to engage in group sexual activity with the participants—the final culmination of the celebration.

While this aspect of worship seems shocking and bizarre to most contemporary people, it was nearly ubiquitous within paganism. The overall purpose of the sacrificial feast was, through sharing a meal, to unite the community to each other and to their gods. The intimacy of these connections was considered to reach an apex in sexual acts. Further, these acts were aimed at ensuring fertility, both among the humans who dwelt in the region and of their crops.

Within ancient paganism, sexual gratification and human reproduction were completely severed. A man had a wife or wives for the purpose of bearing his children. His sexual desire, however, was seen as a bodily need or function, like relieving oneself, eating, or drinking. It was merely one more human appetite to be fulfilled wherever he pleased—with young men, other women, prostitutes, or slaves. Telling one of these ancient pagans that he ought only to have sexual relations with one wife would be like telling him to eat only food that she had cooked.

The pagan view of sexuality explains several features of the teaching of the Scriptures. Throughout the Bible, human sexuality, marriage, and reproduction are drawn back together and united. This union leads to a very different view of the purpose of sexuality as a vital part of marriage directly connected, but not limited, to childbearing. In many biblical texts, the pagans' ritual use of sexuality also tends to unite condemnations both of idolatry and of sexual immorality.[1] These

---

1   For example, Leviticus 18:21–23.

are not just two grievous sins; they are two sins that were intimately related in the life of the ancient world. The view of human sexuality described in the Scriptures would become a major point of distinction between Israel and her neighbors. Christianity spread this view of sexuality to the world, and it was a unique and transformative element of the Christian Faith.

BALAAM AND ISRAEL'S TEMPTATION

ISRAEL'S EXPERIENCE AT PEOR IS described in Numbers 25. Though Balaam, son of Beor, is not mentioned in the chapter, this episode serves as the conclusion of the arc of Balaam's interactions with Israel. In the preceding chapters Balak, the king of Moab, hired Balaam as a prophet to curse Israel for him. After a run-in with the Angel of the Lord and being upbraided by his own donkey, Balaam made repeated attempts to curse Israel but repeatedly announced prophetic blessings instead. This angered Balak and allowed Israel to pass through Moabite territory without incident until they arrived at Peor.

Balaam is a figure now known from extra-biblical evidence to have been important in Moabite religious circles. In 1967, an inscription dated to about 800 BC was found at Deir Alla in Jordan. It tells a story involving a series of visions of the gods received by Balaam, son of Beor. These visions have no direct connections to the text of Numbers or anywhere else in the Scriptures other than involving a prophet in the Transjordan with precisely that name. The Moabite inscription presents Balaam as a prophet of Chemosh, Shaggar, and Shemesh, gods associated with the sun, the moon, and the planet Venus, regarded at the time as the morning star. These three deities represent the primary deities of Moab. The inscription also represents other lesser members of the divine council.

Balaam, then, was a known Moabite hero and champion of their gods who, here in the text of Numbers, attempts to enter into a sort of contest with Moses, the prophet of Yahweh the God of Israel. The episode with his donkey reveals that the animal's insight into the spiritual world is superior to his master's. When Balaam attempts to tap into the power of his gods to issue a curse, instead the true God overpowers him. Through this experience, however, Balaam learns something important: that Israel is invincible when she is faithful to her God. Though defeated, he imparts this insight to Balak, the king and his employer, before he goes.

It is not a coincidence that the Israelites were then lured into the worship of Baal and consorting with shrine prostitutes. It was a setup. Later in the text, Numbers makes it explicit that it was on Balaam's advice that Balak enlisted the priests of the high place at Peor (31:16). In a certain irony, Balaam has learned the lesson that Israel so often in her history failed to learn. When she is faithful, she is, with God, unstoppable; when she is unfaithful to God, then defeat and destruction are imminent. Balaam weaponized this understanding. For this crime, he would eventually be captured and executed by the Israelites (31:8).

Balaam is remembered in Jewish and Christian tradition as a sort of anti-Moses—a paradigm of the false prophet, the heretic, and the religious leader who uses his knowledge and abilities against the people. Philo presents Balaam as a sophist and a heretic, but Josephus presents him as the most powerful prophet of the nations. Josephus appears to be focused on Balaam's abilities as a prophet and his expertise, though he is quick to point out the wickedness of Balaam's use of that power, skill, and insight. In Jewish tradition, Balaam serves as proof of God's justice. When God gave Moses as a prophet to Israel, He gave the nations a powerful prophet as well, leaving them without excuse when they and their prophet remained in sin.

In the New Testament, when Balaam appears, it is always in reference to the way in which he led Israel into sin at Baal-Peor. Second Peter and Jude connect apostate and false Christians to Balaam and those who followed his ways at Peor (2:15 and 1:11, respectively). They are grouped here with other rebels, sinners, and heretics like Cain and Korah from the Torah. In the Book of Revelation, St. John makes an even more direct connection: He compares the leaders within the Christian community at Pergamon to Balaam and his actions at Peor (2:14). These leaders have permitted—if not encouraged—members of the community to eat food offered to idols and to participate in sexual immorality. They are, essentially, doing the same thing as Balaam.

By joining themselves in worship to Baal at Peor through sacrificial and sexual ritual, the Israelites bring about dire consequences for the entire community. Immediately after the sin of the people, led by elders of clans in various Israelite tribes, Moses receives the command that those who have participated must be cut off from the community—either exiled or put to death. Because of their participation in these rituals, a plague strikes the Israelite camp. By the time the plague is lifted, it had killed twenty-four thousand people. The fierceness and destruction of the plague are directly tied to the fact that the Israelite leadership did not cut off the participants from the community as God had commanded.

Because of the prominence of the participants in this wickedness, the weakness of the Israelite leadership in taking action against it, and likely other factors, nothing was done. The idolatry and fornication were allowed to continue. It reached the point that not only was it happening at the high place, a site devoted to pagan ritual, but it had spilled over into the Israelite camp itself. Finally, Zimri, the son of a clan chief in the tribe of Simeon, paraded a shrine prostitute—the daughter of a Midianite tribal chief—past the Israelite assembly, Moses, and the tabernacle. Phinehas, the grandson of Aaron, the high priest, was the one to finally act. He took a spear and executed both the man and the woman (Num. 25:7–8).

The plague lifted immediately. As a reward for his taking action, God promised the high priesthood to Phinehas for himself and his line in perpetuity. Meanwhile, Israel was ordered to make war against the Midianites, some of whom had previously been friendly toward Israel, because of their complicity in Israel's seduction. Phinehas thereby became the symbol for future generations of zeal—specifically, zeal for the purity of the sanctuary and people of God.

UNREPENTANT SIN AND THE COMMUNITY

ONE OF THE IMPORTANT ROLES of the priesthood is the preservation of this purity. As modern people consider this story and others like it, we tend to identify with the sinful. We are, after all, sinners and would greatly fear the kind of consequences not only described but prescribed here for our sins. But the original readers had a very different view. They did not consider it from an individual perspective or identify with particular people in the story. Rather, they saw a story about the consequences of unrepentant sin for the community that tolerates it and allows it to fester.

While contemporary people value minding their own business, being open-minded, and pursuing an ethos of "live and let live," the reality is that sin has effects. Sin affects not only those who engage in it and become enslaved by it; a person's sin affects them, those close to them, and the whole community. Ignoring sin, especially serious sin that is publicly known and not repented of, shows a lack of compassion for the sinner, their loved ones, and the community as a whole. Pain, suffering, and difficulty all increase when their cause is not dealt with.

A person, then, who steps in to confront the sin and correct the sinner is blessed because that is the person who truly loves the one lost in sin. This confrontation is not out of a desire to punish or ostra-cize those who are guilty of particular transgressions. Rather, it is aimed at repentance and restoration. Excommunication—being cut off from the community—is always a last resort. Even the last resort, however, carries with it the hope that the one cut off might repent, return, and be restored. Within the community of the Church, this is a responsibility given to her bishops and delegated in many cases to the priesthood. When all else fails, however, it is the responsibility of every Christian to correct his brother in mercy.

Baal in the Psalms

THROUGHOUT PSALMS AND IN THE Book of Job, the Scriptures interact with Baal and his worship in a variety of ways. These interac-tions are in poetic form, rather than telling stories or presenting Isra-el's history. Their power and effect lie in the way in which traditional language is applied or reapplied to the God of Israel, Baal, and the wor-shipers of each. Understanding these more subtle interactions requires a close attention to details such as the choice of words and images.

Poetic elements commonly used to refer to Baal in Syrian and Canaanite literature are ascribed to Yahweh the God of Israel. The use of this language takes a variety of forms. In some cases, elements of narrative from Baal stories are recast or even inverted, based on the presence of the true God. In other cases, elements that ascribe power or praise to Baal are instead used to attribute that power or give that praise to Yahweh, their rightful recipient. Other psalms, and Job, make use of Kaoskampf motifs in describing the creation of the world.

Modern scholars often cite these biblical texts as evidence that Yah-weh is simply another name for Baal and that Israel's religion emerged from Baal worship—or some similar view. The logic behind this argument is dubious. The same scholars hold that the Hebrew Scriptures achieved their final form after the exile, at which point Israel was, at least in some sense, monotheistic, and that they were edited accordingly. These verses, then, are considered to be places where the final editors "got sloppy" and let the "secret truth" slip through. This sort of conspiracy thinking is based on very little evidence.

This is especially true when one considers that the reappropriation of another culture's religious ideas and motifs for polemical purposes was very common in the ancient Near East. When one pagan cult didn't wholly subsume another, as when a nation had a rival of roughly equivalent power, it was common for that nation to promote their deity or deities and demote those of the rival. If one rival ever fell to the other, the defeat would be made official by assimilating the deities of the conquered nation as low-ranking members of the conqueror's divine council.

PSALM 18/17

PSALM 18/17 IS A GOOD example of a Hebrew psalm that takes the language of Israel's neighbors traditionally associated with Baal and applies it to Yahweh the God of Israel. The overall theme of the psalm really becomes clear only in the final verses. This is a psalm about the deliverance of the Davidic king of Israel from enemy nations. These enemy nations, by and large, throughout this period worshiped Baal. Yahweh's deliverance of the king and Israel itself from Baal's followers prompts the author's promise to speak of Yahweh among the nations—to seek to bring them to the worship of the true God (vv. 49–50). The true enemies are not the people who populate those nations, but Baal, the demonic power who has enslaved them.

This psalm mixes together two sets of symbols associated with Baal. Verses 4–6 reference the imagery of Baal as the lord of the dead.

This language is not directly applied to the God of Israel; rather, the power of the God of Israel is contrasted to this power of Baal's and portrayed as superior. The underworld itself, let alone its would-be ruler, shakes at the coming of the God of Israel (v. 7). The God of Israel is more powerful than death itself.

Psalm 18/17 also takes the storm-god language used for Baal by his cult and applies it to the God of Israel instead (vv. 9–14). For the psalmist, it is Yahweh who commands the thunder and lightning, who brings the rain in its seasons, and controls the powers of nature. As already discussed, this is not because Yahweh is a storm god per se but because Baal is powerless. The most important attribute applied here to the God of Israel has nothing to do with rain or fertility; rather, it is the fact that He, not Baal, defeated Yam, the sea (vv. 15–16). The God of Israel is the One who overcame chaos and created the world and everything in it, including Baal.

This psalm cedes to Baal the power of death, but only to an extent. Yahweh is not a god of death or the underworld per se. He reigns on high and is above all created things (vv. 6–9). On the other hand, when the power of death stands opposed to His purposes and His anointed one has been seized by death and nearly overcome, He strikes with a terrible vengeance (vv. 46–48). Death and its forces in the world, identified here with Baal rather than Yahweh, are unable to withstand even a moment of His power. Death is powerless to resist the God of Israel.

PSALM 24/23

THE OPENING LINES OF PSALM 24/23 directly address the fact that language attributed by his cult to Baal is properly given as praise to the God of Israel. The world and everything in it belong to Yahweh because it is He who has created the world and put it in order. It is He who has defeated chaos in the persons of the seas and the rivers—that is, the primordial chaos gods Yam and Nahar (vv. 1–2). Baal's cult praised him for a great victory that Yahweh actually accomplished, and, by the way, He prevailed without resistance or a need to engage in battle.

Verse 3 begins a sort of sarcastic address to Baal: "Who is it who is able to ascend the mountain of God where the Most High dwells?" It is not a rebel like Baal. Rather, the one who is pure and clean, who is holy and righteous, receives the blessings of the Most High God. The psalmist leaves open the question of whether he is describing a general type of person who is blessed or a particular righteous one who is being contrasted with the rebellious figure of Baal.

The central portion of the psalm describes the one who is able to ascend the mountain of God, and the final portion describes a descent where Yahweh the God of Israel goes into battle. Specifically, He engages in siege warfare against the ancient gates of the underworld. In this psalm, again Baal is located in the underworld, enshrined in his palace. As the Divine King comes to deal with Baal in his domain of the dead, He taunts Baal. In the version of this encounter in the Baal Cycle, Baal rallies his fellow gods to join his revolution by crying out, "Lift up your heads, O ye gods." Yahweh, however, needs no assistance to deal with Baal. He therefore tells the gates of Sheol or Hades to prepare for their own destruction.

Psalm 24/23 speaks of a day when Yahweh Himself, in person, will destroy the gates of the city of the dead. Once the gates are destroyed, the so-called lord of the dead will be defeated, and the city will be plundered. For this reason, this psalm has been used throughout the history of the Church, both in interpretation and liturgically, as prophetic. Psalm 24/23 is speaking before the time of the descent of Christ into Hades, when he will free humanity held captive by death. This liberation represents the defeat and destruction of the one who wields the power of death (Heb. 2:14).

PSALM 29/28

THE OPENING OF PSALM 29/28 is directed not to human worshipers but to the sons of God. It calls upon the powers of heaven—in its original context, "the gods"—to worship Yahweh the God of Israel. We are likely more comfortable referring to these as angelic and demonic beings. But critically important is the fact that Yahweh is not here presented as one of them—even as the greatest of their number. Rather, He is the God of gods. The author, traditionally David, is asserting before the world that Yahweh is to the gods of the nations as those gods are to humans. He is of an entirely different order as their Creator and ultimately their judge.

To reinforce what is being communicated here, the attributes and feats that neighboring cultures associated with Baal and his ilk are ascribed to Yahweh instead. They are presented as the reason why all these lesser, created divine beings must now give worship to the true God. In this psalm, it is specifically the voice of the Lord that thunders, brings fertility and new life to the world, and defeats and overwhelms the forces of nature that are opposed to humanity. Unlike the sagas of the pagan gods, the God of Israel does not have to exert Himself or enter into combat with any other force. None is comparable to Him. He speaks, and the storms, the mountains, the sea, and the wild beasts all obey.

PSALM 48/47

PSALM 48/47 IS A PSALM praising Zion, the hill in Jerusalem on which the temple sits, as well as the city itself. The temple is here depicted as the palace of the Most High God. This makes Zion the mountain of God, and Yahweh presides over the divine council on top of it. This hymn of praise for the temple, the mountain, and the city is ultimately a veneration of these earthly realities because they communicate the glory of the God of Israel. The psalm contains a single reference to the Baal cult in a rather counterintuitive way: Verse 2 describes Zion as a mountain "in the far north."

The Baal cult held that Baal presided over the divine council on Mount Zaphon, which means "the mountain of the North." Obviously, Jerusalem is not in the far north by anyone's definition, so it is important to remember that the identification of the mountain of the gods with a particular physical mountain was not meant entirely literally in the modern sense of the word. People had been to the top of Mount Olympus, Mount Zaphon, Mount Hermon, and other candidates. They did not find tents occupied by literal humanoid gods there. Nonetheless, ancient people made this spiritual identification.

Psalm 48/47 is not attempting to describe the location of Jerusalem in physical geography. Rather, in terms of spiritual geography, the psalm identifies Zion in Jerusalem as the mountain of God. The psalm is not asserting that Zion is Zaphon or vice versa. Rather, the psalm presents Mount Zion in Jerusalem as the true mountain from which the true God presides over the entire creation. This implies, polemically, that Mount Zaphon is a false mountain and Baal a false god. His claims are untrue. Only the God of Israel can rightly make such claims.

PSALM 68/67

PSALM 68/67 DESCRIBES THE GOD of Israel leading a procession and calls worshipers to join in. This procession, however, is actually that of a war band going forth into battle. Specifically, Yahweh is going to war with Bashan (vv. 15–17). Bashan is likely best known in the Hebrew Bible as the land ruled over by the giant king Og, who was defeated by the Israelites on the way into the land of Canaan (Num. 21; Deut. 3). Og is presented as being in the line of the Anakim, the giants like the Nephilim of the era before the Flood.

He is a perpetrator of abominations and a human representative of spiritual evil.

Bashan was located in the north, and the Psalm explicitly refers to the mountain there, believed to be the home of Baal (vv. 15–16). This area, therefore, is portrayed as the realm of the evil spiritual forces arrayed against God's people. It is the land of the dead in which they have been taken captive, representing the underworld (vv. 20–23). The psalm praises the God of Israel for being victorious over these forces in advance of that victory. So certain is the defeat of the enemies that the victory can be celebrated on the way to the battle.

It is not a coincidence that later Christianity would pick up this psalm to describe Christ's defeat of the spiritual forces of evil and death itself. Already within the pages of the New Testament, St. Paul quotes verse 18 to describe Christ's victory over these powers and His taking of spoils, which he shares with the people of God (Eph. 4:8). The opening verses of Psalm 68/67 are used liturgically in the Orthodox Church as part of the celebration of Pascha, based on reading this psalm in the same way.

PSALM 89/88

PSALM 89/88 COMBINES ELEMENTS OF several of the psalms already discussed. It presents Yahweh the God of Israel as presiding over the council of the gods. It also makes clear that none of these holy ones is in remotely the same category as the true God. He is, in fact, their God (vv. 6–7). This psalm, however, is more than a general statement about the God of Israel as God of gods or about the deficiencies of the pagan gods.

As the psalm progresses, it becomes increasingly clear that its argument is directed to one set of gods and one claimant to being a king of the gods. Yahweh is said to be the One in command of Yam, the sea (v. 9). Again He rules over it by speaking, not by having to battle him. He is said to have crushed Rahav, one of Yam's dragons (v. 9). Both the heavens and the underworld belong to Yahweh (v. 11). He is the One who created the north and the south (v. 12). This is not just a reference to the ends of the physical earth. The mention of Tabor and Hermon as mountains refers back to the opening of the psalm, which describes the heavens, the home of the gods. The divine beings thought to dwell in these places, angelic or demonic, are also creations of the one Creator God.

The position the psalmist takes is not that Baal and his ilk do not exist. Rather, they are taken to be legitimate spiritual powers created by, and subservient in ways to, the true God, the God of Israel. Nevertheless, Baal is presented as being at odds with the true God, his Creator. This opposition takes the form of the worship and credit ascribed to him for the deeds and power that belong to Yahweh. A time will come, however, when he will be forced to admit this and give glory to the Most High God.

PSALM 104/103

PSALM 104/103, WELL KNOWN FOR its place in the Vespers service, is a poetic meditation on God's act of creation. His creation of the world through His command, rather than contest, repeatedly references elements of Baal stories in order to make this contrast clearer. The true God creates without struggle or battle; the creation simply obeys Him and springs into being. The use of Baal language here had likely now become typical. It is Yahweh who rides upon the clouds of heaven and overcomes the sea (v. 3). The waters therefore answer His commands (vv. 7–9). He does not engage in an epic battle with Leviathan; He created her and plays with her like a pet (v. 26). Not only the initial creation of the world and the life in it are the work of Yahweh, but the ongoing cycle of life, fertility, and creation all come from His hand.

Job

INCLUDED HERE BECAUSE OF THE genre is a description from the Book of Job of the creation of the world in poetic form. At the end of the book, God appears to Job to respond to his questions, claims, and complaints and also to respond to the claims of Job's friends. The general tenor of this response is God calling into question whether it is really possible for Job to receive the answers he wants. Is Job capable of understanding the complexities of the workings of the world and of history? At what point does Job merely need, in humility, to trust in the God who created Him and in His wisdom and justice?

AN "ALTERNATIVE" CREATION STORY?

TO MAKE THIS POINT, GOD gives a poetic description of the creation of the world, repeatedly asking Job if he can understand and explain how God did it. This description, however, contains marked differences from the text of Genesis 1—2. Based on the differences, scholars during a certain era commonly presented the Job account as an "alternative" Creation story from Israel competing with that in Genesis. During that period, many scholars believed the Book of Job to be far older than the final form of the Book of Genesis. They therefore claimed that the version of the story in Job, which has connections to the Kaoskampf stories of the surrounding nations, was the original Israelite Creation story and that Genesis was a much later revision. This argument generally is no longer made, however, as scholars now commonly date the Book of Job to a much later period—later at least than some layers of the Book of Genesis. Therefore, even skeptical scholars acknowledge that the Genesis version of the story and Job's are contemporary in a very rough sense.

BEYOND HUMAN COMPREHENSION

THE FACT THAT JOB IN its canonical Hebrew form is fully integrated with the rest of the Hebrew Scriptures attests that the earliest readers did not think these stories were incompatible. Each must have served a different function that merited the preservation of both, even though these stories are presented in radically different contexts. Within the story of Job, the entire point of God relating this information to him is Job's inability to understand it. God is describing something in human words in order to show that God's act of Creation is beyond human comprehension. That the telling of the story mimics various stories of human invention about the creation of the world, therefore, makes sense. God essentially asks, "You say that this is how it happened. What does that even mean?"

Within the telling, many of the tropes are drawn from Syro-Canaanite stories regarding Baal that should now be familiar from the Psalms. Job 38 describes God overcoming the power of the sea. It is the God of Israel who leads the procession of the constellations through the stars, which humans believe govern their lives and history. It is Yahweh who controls the storms and the rain. Though Job is cowed by the account, God continues in chapter 40 to describe the great beasts of myth, and in chapter 41 the Behemoth and the Leviathan. Yahweh domesticates Behemoth, the great bull of heaven, like standard cattle. The God of Israel catches Leviathan, the great chaos serpent, like a fish with a hook in its mouth. All these mighty acts are the province of the true Most High God. It is presumptuous for humans to try to speak of them. Even more so, it is blasphemy to attribute them to some other spiritual power.

Jezebel

LIKELY THE MOST WELL-KNOWN BIBLICAL story involving Baal and his followers is the story of the life of the Prophet Elijah—specifically, the opposition he faced throughout his life. Elijah's prophetic career is described in 1 Kings 17 through 2 Kings 2 (3 and 4 Kingdoms in the Greek). At the time of the composition of the history recorded in these books, the worship of Baal was still common, so little background description is given. It is assumed that readers will be familiar with these events. While the stories surrounding Elijah and his contest with the prophets of Baal are certainly understandable in translation, an understanding of Baal and the Baal cult sheds additional light on the narrative.

JEROBOAM'S NEW RELIGION

BAAL WORSHIP BECAME A PART of the official religion of the Northern Kingdom of Israel during the Omride dynasty, specifically through the marriage of Omri's son, Ahab, to Jezebel. Before Ahab's accession to the throne, the official religion of Israel had been the worship of Yahweh, though in a form far removed from that prescribed by the Torah. Jeroboam I, son of Nebat, had established this religion centered around two shrines in Bethel and Dan at the northern and southern ends of his newly independent kingdom. He had constructed his own priesthood to serve at these shrines. Many, but not all of them, were Levite, though not of the high priestly line of Judah.

Jeroboam designed this religion deliberately after the split from the tribes of Judah and Benjamin. The temple to Yahweh had been constructed by Solomon in Jerusalem, and Solomon's death was the moment when Jeroboam rallied the other tribes to break away. His people's practice of continuing to make pilgrimages and send tithes to the sanctuary in the Southern Kingdom represented a threat to his rule. He built his religion around familiar pagan worship structures while maintaining the name of Yahweh in order to make a pretense of continuity. At the same time, he also appealed to the common, rural people's religious sensibilities. The center points of the two shrines were golden calves, and worship was offered to them.

Because of these pagan worship structures, the Northern Kingdom was more tolerant of religious diversity, almost by default. While in the cities the royal cult likely prevailed, in rural areas, high places and other sacred sites related to Baal and other regional deities were tolerated. Only Yahwism as practiced in the Southern Kingdom of Judah was strictly off limits from the perspective of the royal house. The official line taken by the government of the Northern Kingdom was that their practice was the original religion of the Israelite people; they stood in direct continuity with the patriarchs who had made Bethel a sacred site.

Jeroboam, who established the Northern Kingdom, also set a pattern regarding her monarch beyond instituting their religion. He was a member of Solomon's court who rebelled against Rehoboam, Solomon's son and heir. The early history of Israel ended up facing a quick succession not only of monarchs but of dynasties, each lasting only two generations. The Omride dynasty was the fourth in the Northern Kingdom, but based on the stability and infrastructure that the founder Omri built, Omri's is in many ways the dynasty that established that kingdom.

OMRI AND JEZEBEL

VERY LITTLE IS SAID ABOUT Omri in the Hebrew Scriptures other than an acknowledgment of his wickedness (1 Kin./3 Kgdms. 16:21–28). Nonetheless, both the history that follows in those Scriptures and the broader history of the ancient Near East reflect his influence.

It was Omri who built the city of Samaria, which would be the capital of Israel for the rest of its existence. He established trade relations throughout the region and was victorious in war against troublesome neighbors, establishing several decades of peace. His name is found in a number of Assyrian inscriptions that, even after the end of his dynasty, refer to Israel as the "House of Omri."

Alliances in the ancient Near East were sealed through royal marriages, and Omri's most important alliance was with the Phoenician king of Tyre. Jezebel, the daughter of Ithobaal I, was married to Omri's son Ahab. Much like Baal, Jezebel's father had seized, rather than inherited, the throne. Ithobaal had been a priest of the goddess Astarte and had murdered Phelles, the previous king, to take the throne. Making alliances with his neighbors was a way for him to cement and legitimize his own power over Tyre, Sidon, and the rest of the Phoenician world. At this, he was largely successful, in that he was able to pass on the kingdom to his own son Baal-Esser II.

As these names suggest, it was critically important to a Phoenician king to associate himself with the king of the Phoenician gods. *Ithobaal* means "with Baal." *Baal-Esser* means, roughly, "Baal is my helper." The meaning of Jezebel's name is unclear, likely because it is a parody of her actual name. In Phoenician inscriptions, we find a feminine name that would be roughly transliterated as "Baal-zebaal." This would mean something like "Baal is lord." *Jezebel*, on the other hand, means, "Where is Baal?" Given that Hebrew biblical authors would be disinclined to profess Baal's lordship, it is entirely possible that they have renamed Jezebel in her biblical appearances. The author of these books does the same with, for example, Ish-Baal, the son of Saul named "man of Baal," by changing his name to Ish-Bosheth, or "man of Shame." The question as to Baal's whereabouts is directly connected to the culmination of the story of Elijah's contest with the followers of Baal.

REPRESSION OF YAHWEH WORSHIP

AHAB ASCENDED THE THRONE IN roughly 875 BC. When he came to power with Jezebel as his leading wife, his father had left him a newly established but thriving kingdom. Based on her position in the narrative, she seems to have taken a great hand in royal policy. With a new capital and a new sense of Israelite identity in the north, Jezebel sought to bring about a religious transformation. Even the Yahwism of Jeroboam was, for the new regime, too close to the religion of the Southern Kingdom, so it would be replaced by Baal worship brought down from Jezebel's homeland in the north.

The level of violence in the repression of Yahwism in Israel seems to have been directly proportional to the allegiance of religious functionaries to the religion of Judah. For most of the cultic officials from Bethel and Dan, let alone tribal elders functioning at high places, this allegiance was next to none, and they seem to have transitioned easily into their new situation. There were, however, communities of prophets physically located in the Northern Kingdom. Unlike priests, these prophets were neither restricted to the tribe of Levi, nor to the temple and its particular rites. They lived communally as families and functioned outside of both monarchy and priesthood as individuals with a direct line to Yahweh the God of Israel. They were instruments through whom God could check the authority of those other institutions and correct them.

Despite not representing any priesthood per se, these prophets were dedicated to the received Mosaic traditions surrounding the temple as well as to the legitimacy of the Levitical priesthood functioning there. Further, they were utterly unbending before any king or royal cult. Jezebel therefore began a purge of these prophets of Yahweh that resulted in their deaths by the hundreds. Those numbers likely include the wives and children of the prophets. A group of roughly one hundred of these prophets and their families was taken in and sheltered by a certain Obadiah, whose name means "servant of Yahweh" (1 Kin. 18:4).

In their place, Jezebel brought in hundreds of prophets of Baal who worked in ways similar to Balaam, son of Beor. They were traveling religious functionaries, not restricted to a particular religious site. These prophets were fully empowered to perform various rituals in the life of the Baal cult but could do so at official shrines, rural high places, or wherever else their services might be required. These were not itinerant preachers bringing a proclamation. Rather, they would travel into a region and perform rituals to bless crops and herds, offering sacrifices and receiving offerings from the local people.

The Baal cult under Ahab and Jezebel, then, was not just a new face on the existing royal cult. Jeroboam's cult was established by the ruler and then enforced on the common people. Jezebel's Baal prophets instead worked to remake Israelite religion from the bottom up. They met and interacted with the people—many if not most of whom by this time had a fundamentally pagan mindset regarding religion—and guided them into Baal worship. While this was a greatly successful approach, as evidenced in the biblical narrative, there was a certain tension within Israelite culture. A historical memory of Yahweh as their God, and Baalism as a foreign cult, still remained.

ELIJAH CONFRONTS THE HOUSE OF AHAB

AS A LEADER AMONG YAHWEH'S surviving prophets, Elijah, whose name means "My God is Yahweh," is the prophet sent to set in motion God's judgment against the house of Ahab and this promotion of false religion. He throws down the gauntlet before Ahab in a manner both direct and simple. Elijah simply tells the king and his court that it will no longer rain in Israel (1 Kin. 17:1). He did not predict a particular length for the drought; he said only that it would last until Yahweh gave the word for the rain to fall again. For three years, it did not rain, and Elijah was protected as he hid from Jezebel, who sought his death.

Because Baal was a storm god, his inability to send rain to provide for the growing of crops and the sustenance of herds and the lives of his own followers is a deadly blow. The very reason for his worship is undermined. Clearly, Baal needs Yahweh's permission before he is able to do anything—if he is, in fact, able to do anything at all. After this three-year demonstration, Elijah returns to confront Ahab a second time (1 Kin. 18:17–19). This time, he calls for a sort of prophetic showdown at Mount Carmel, one of the high places in the central region of the Northern Kingdom. This location allows for the largest possible audience of the people. On one side would be Elijah and his God, Yahweh. On the other side would be the roughly 450 prophets of Baal and four hundred prophets of the goddess Asherah, whom Jezebel had brought into Israel.

This showdown also was designed to strike at the heart of the conception of Baal that his worshipers held. The Baal Cycle describes Baal as the one who wields the fire from heaven—the thunderbolt. While the rain, related to fertility, was associated with the favor Baal's followers sought from him, the thunderbolt was associated with his power and wrath. Elijah had shown that Baal did not control the rain. Elijah now arranges a challenge to show that he did not have the power of the thunderbolt either.

On the mountain, Elijah sets up an altar to Yahweh where an ancient one, from the period of the patriarchs, had been. He uses twelve stones for the twelve tribes of Israel (vv. 30–31), a reminder that the unity of the tribes in the worship of Yahweh was to supersede the present political divisions of north and south. The hundreds of prophets of Baal were allowed to use the existing high-place altar. Each side had a bull to offer in sacrifice, but no fire to ignite the altar. They were to call out to their respective deities and see who answered with lightning to burn the offering and receive the sacrifice (vv. 21–24).

Elijah engages in significant bravado during this confrontation. As the prophets of Baal become increasingly desperate in their ritual practice, resorting to scarification and bleeding themselves nearly to death to try to get Baal's attention, Elijah suggests that Baal might be on vacation or taking a bathroom break. When the time comes for Elijah to call upon the God of Israel in prayer, he has several massive clay jugs of water poured over his altar, the firewood, and the sacrifice before beginning (vv. 32–35). After his brief prayer, the lightning comes and not only ignites the offering, it incinerates it along with the wood and the altar, and vaporizes the water.

Elijah then takes up a sword and, along with the galvanized Israelites who had seen this display of the power of Yahweh, slaughters Baal's prophets. After the death of hundreds of Yahweh's prophets at their hands, this is rough justice. Ahab would certainly not be the instrument of God's justice in this matter, though that was his role as king. The task fell instead to his prophet. To emphasize the point, a massive rainstorm then rolls in from the sea, ending the drought.

DEATH AND SUCCESSION

WHEN HER HUSBAND TELLS HER what had happened, Jezebel receives the news not with repentance but with an oath to her gods that she would have her revenge by killing Elijah (19:1–2). This lack of repentance would bring about the end of the line of Ahab and the Omride dynasty in the north. Jezebel herself died and was eaten by dogs, and Ahab was killed in a military disaster. His successor died less than two years after receiving the throne when Jehu rose up and killed him, making himself king. Jehu set out to purge Ahab's family from Israel, massacring anyone with a claim to the throne. He also rolled back Jezebel's religious transformation, returning Israel to the royal cult established by Jeroboam.

The last surviving member of Ahab's family was Athaliah, his daughter, whom he had married to Jehoram, the king of the Southern Kingdom of Judah, in order to ensure peace on his southern border. Jehu's massacre of Ahab's family included Jehoram himself, and Athaliah, from her position as queen mother within the Davidic monarchy, seized the throne for six years. During this period, she attempted to move her now-dead mother's Baal cult into Judah to displace the worship of Yahweh there and to solidify her power by murdering every member she could find of the line of David. Jehoash, an heir to the throne, survived Athaliah's killings and was later crowned king of Judah. At that point Jehoash's bodyguards dispatched her, finally ending the Omride line and the direct influence of the Phoenician Baal cult in Israel and Judah.

The Devil's Fall

THE PROPHETIC LITERATURE OF THE Old Testament represents yet another genre. The prophetic literature speaks directly to and reveals spiritual realities that lie behind the material world, its players, and events. Three key passages of Scripture describe the fall of a divine figure that comes to be referred to in the Second Temple period as *o diabolos*, the Devil. This being, a member of Yahweh's divine council, rebels against the true God and His authority and, in return, is thrown down into the underworld. Even in this brief summary, one can see the parallel arc to that of the Baal Cycle. Baal begins as a vassal of the most high god and ends up as a denizen of the underworld. This story is portrayed in the Baal Cycle as a series of victories for which Baal ought to be praised. But in the Hebrew Scriptures this is, rather, an arc of horrifying defeat and an object lesson regarding rebellion and sin. The Devil is a figure who seeks the destruction of humanity; he is not one to be supplicated in order for humanity to receive blessings.

Not only do these Scripture passages, in their movement, represent an inversion of the flow of the Baal Cycle, but they also draw heavily upon imagery from different aspects of the Baal cult. The first describes the origin of sin and death in the world; the other two are directed toward human kings from nations that serve Baal in different localizations. They warn these human rulers of the fate that befell the being that their society worships and serves—a fate that his followers will inevitably share.

GENESIS 3

MOST CHRISTIANS OF THE MODERN era have been taught to read Genesis 3 in a particular way—focusing on the transgression of humanity's first parents and the result of sin and death being brought into the world. While this way of reading the story has value, it does not exhaust what the passage has to teach. Of particular importance to the present discussion is the figure of the serpent, who also suffers a fall within the narrative of this chapter. Neither the Book of Genesis, nor the Torah as a whole, refers to this serpent by the names *Satan* or *the Devil*. However, the serpent as a spiritual entity, together with the image of a divine rebel later in the Hebrew Scriptures, forms the basis of the figure later described by those names.

A certain school of thought wants to see the serpent of Genesis 3 as merely a talking animal. This turns his arc in the chapter into a Kipling-style "just-so story" of how the snake lost its legs. Out of context, as with nearly any other passage of Scripture, there is no way to prove otherwise. However, the way in which this text has been received historically by the rest of the Hebrew Scriptures, by later Judaism, and by Christianity disagrees with this naturalistic understanding. The woodenly literal reading that sees him as a talking animal is modern and unattested in ancient interpretation.

The word here translated as "serpent" is itself a sort of wordplay. The Hebrew consonants "n-ch-sh" can be vocalized or pronounced in several different ways. Depending on this pronunciation, it could be the word for a snake, serpent, or even dragon. It could be the adjective that means "shining," like brass. It could also be a word for subtlety or deceit. Different elements of the story reflect these variations in meaning, such as his introduction as the cleverest of the beasts. Put together, these meanings describe a spiritual power, serpentine in nature like one of the seraphim, who is shining and devious.[2]

This being attempts to seduce the first woman into partaking of the knowledge of good and evil—knowledge for which she is not ready. He promises that doing so will make her like him and his fellow powers. Contained within this promise is the central notion of later paganism: To worship and serve a spiritual power is to become like it—to acquire its powers. The serpent offers the woman the opportunity to follow and thereby become like him, rather than being faithful to the true God who created her and thereby becoming like Him in time. She follows the serpent's prodding and leads the first man to do the same. In seeking the worship, and thereby the destruction, of the crown of God's creation, humanity, the serpent has rebelled against his own Creator.

As a result, it is not only the man and woman who face the consequences of their action but the serpent as well. God had made the serpent and his fellow angelic beings a little higher than the creatures

---

2   The word *seraph* is a loan word from the Egyptian *seraf*, which refers to a serpent. Winged serpents are the common way in which seraphim were depicted in ancient Israel. In Egyptian religion, these beings guarded the thrones of the gods, accounting for the cobra and other serpent motifs in Egyptian iconography and royal burials.

who live upon the earth, whom He created on the sixth day. Now, because of what he had done, the serpent would be beneath all of them (v. 14). He is not only banished from his heavenly place but from the earth as well, to the regions under the earth.

Ancient people knew that snakes did not eat dirt. They had seen them eat birds and rodents. The dust that the serpent would henceforth eat is the same dust—the same word in the text—as the dust from which humans were made and to which they would return when they died (v. 19). The serpent is not only banished to the underworld, he is made the eater of the dead, their devourer.

The curse levied against the serpent, however, gets worse. Even this kingdom of dust and ashes will not be his permanently. His ultimate defeat will come through one of the woman's descendants who will one day crush his head (v. 15). This is a prophecy not only of judgment against the serpent but of the defeat and destruction of death itself. Though subtle in this first appearance, the narrative of Baal as victorious in the underworld is here inverted. To dwell among the dead, propaganda aside, is defeat, even if one claims to rule there. It is a defeat that presages oncoming destruction.

EZEKIEL

YAHWEH THE GOD OF ISRAEL gives the Prophet Ezekiel a series of oracles to speak about the impending judgment of the nations. These are not generalized; each is directed against a particular nation. One of these nations is the Phoenician Empire, whose capital, Tyre, is addressed in Ezekiel 28 along with neighboring Sidon. The oracle opens with a prophecy against the human king of Tyre, referred to as the city's "prince." Though he is just a man like any other, he has claimed to be a god. The true God tells him that he will die like any other man and be cast down into the pit, the abyss in the depths of the sea.

After this pronouncement of doom against Tyre's human ruler, the text turns to another figure beginning in verse 11. Here it is not the prince of Tyre who is addressed and condemned for making himself out to be a god. Instead, this figure is addressed as the "king" of Tyre and described as having in some sense been a god. He is said to have been present in Eden (v. 13) and carved of gold and precious stones like an angelic being. He is said to have been a guardian cherub (v. 14). He is said to have walked on the mountain of God in the midst of the other spiritual powers.

If this latter prophecy is also addressed to the human king, then the two oracles are directly contradictory. The prince of Tyre is chided for calling himself a god and claiming he sat among the gods (v. 2), and the human king of Tyre is said to have done exactly that. His doom is assured; he will die as all other men do, though his death will be a violent one.

But the doom of the "king" of Tyre is spoken of as having already happened: God has already cast him out from the mountain of God and destroyed him (v. 16). He has been punished for his overweening pride (v. 17). As a telling detail, the king of Tyre is said to have been reduced to ashes in the sight of all the nations of the world (v. 18). This last element is key to connecting this figure with that of the serpent. Both represent would-be rebels, à la Baal, whose descent to the underworld was anything but a successful revolution.

The distinction between the human prince and the demonic king of Tyre is intended to separate the human deceived by the demonic power from the demonic power itself. Just as the serpent, Eve, and Adam are addressed separately regarding the consequences of their actions, so here the misled, wicked human is addressed separately from his spiritual corruptor. The language used in both oracles is similar, reflecting the fact that the human king has become the son or image of the being he worships. This also means that he will share that being's fate.

The god worshiped at Tyre and seen as its ruler was, of course, Baal. In Genesis, out of his envy of humanity and human destiny, the serpent was placed beneath not only humanity but also all the creatures who dwell upon the earth. Here, Baal is cursed for having deceived the nations in general, and Tyre in particular, into worshiping him. He has already been thrown down; now he will face humiliation and destruction. Those nations that were tricked into glorifying him will see him laid low and will mock and scorn him instead. Humans from those very nations will be among his judges.

ISAIAH

AS WITH THE PROPHET EZEKIEL, God gives Isaiah oracles to pronounce against the nations opposed to Israel. In the midst of these oracles, in Isaiah 14 one is directed to the king of Babylon. The use of the "king" terminology as in Ezekiel makes this section stand out from the others. Additionally, the surrounding oracles are directed toward nations, but Isaiah 14:3–21 is directed toward a singular figure. It prophesies judgment toward the king's sons—here, the people of Babylon who have been deceived by him. Otherwise, it describes the doom of this spiritual power that stands behind Babylon, both the empire long dead by the time of Isaiah and the Neo-Babylonian Empire soon to rise. Later, when the Neo-Babylonian Empire arose, Baal entered their worship as Bel, who was eventually assimilated into the figure of Marduk, Babylon's native rebellious divine son.

The figure here described has ruled the nations in anger, implying that he ought to have governed or shepherded them in some other way (vv. 5–6). He has been the cause of idolatrous worship that will cease when he is destroyed (v. 8). In the central part of the oracle, the actual descent of this spiritual being who is cast into the underworld is described in terms familiar to the Baal cult. As he sinks into Sheol, the Rephaim—the ancient kings—rise up to meet him as they do all the dead (v. 9). He has become just like those whom he deceived into trying to become like him (v. 10). He now has maggots as a bed and a blanket of worms and stench (v. 11). It is a long way down from the pinnacle to the pit.

The second half of this prophecy makes it clear that his descent began from the heights, not from earth, as it would be for a human king. This figure is compared to the morning star, one of the three great lights, along with the sun and the moon (v. 12). In translating this verse into Latin, St. Jerome coined the name *Lucifer,* which became a traditional name for the Devil. The text of Isaiah, however, identifies this figure quite clearly as Baal. In his pride, he tried to make himself the Most High, meaning that he wanted to sit on the mount of assembly, the mountain of the gods, and preside in the far reaches of the north (v. 13). This was, of course, the exact plan of Baal in the Baal Cycle, complete with the mountain of assembly being identified with Mount Zaphon.

Contrary to the arc of the Baal Cycle, however, Isaiah makes clear that this rebellion was a failure that resulted in Baal being confined to Sheol. While he was able to cause great chaos and destruction in the world of men and among the nations whom he deceived into following and worshiping him, his final fate would be even worse than theirs (vv. 16–20). His rebellion has failed utterly, and he has not achieved even one of his goals.

These three passages in the Hebrew Scriptures present a different picture of the being worshiped as Baal. If the descriptions given by God through His prophets are correct, which of course they are, then the Baal Cycle is fake news and deceptive propaganda. It is a narrative that tries to turn defeats into victories by claiming a victory that didn't happen. While the nations surrounding Israel may follow this figure now, he is doomed, and they will see through his lies.

The Enthronement of the Son of Man

DANIEL 7 CONTAINS ONE OF the most well-known prophetic visions in the Old Testament. Like Genesis 3, it is commonly read from certain theological angles. This chapter, and the latter part of Daniel in general, are often interpreted unhelpfully by those seeking a chart or road map for the future and the end of the world. More importantly, this text describes the Son of Man, an apocalyptic figure who would come to be associated with the coming Messiah who will judge the world (e.g., Matt 26:64; Mark 14:62). This makes it an important text for Christology, especially for understanding that the New Testament writers and their contemporaries understood the Messiah to be a divine figure.

Moving past the future influence of this text, it is worth looking at the imagery and the texts that informed it. The early portion of the chapter makes use of now-familiar symbolism. Several beasts or cherubim, representing the spiritual powers behind a series of empires, emerge before Daniel one by one. These have long been taken to represent the Neo-Babylonian, Persian, Seleucid (Greek), and Roman empires. The final beast is at once the worst of them all and reflects the power behind the other beasts—that is, the rebellious spiritual power behind the other rebellious spiritual powers.

Following the defeat of that great beast, a tableau unfolds in which a figure called "one like a Son of Man" is enthroned. The thrones of the divine council are set up, and the Ancient of Days, the Most High God, takes His seat (v. 9). The council convenes to judge the beasts and their followers from among the nations. Then the Son of Man arrives. Though he appears to Daniel to be human, he comes riding on the clouds of heaven (v. 13). This is not just any Baal language that we have seen elsewhere attributed to Yahweh; "the cloud rider" was one of Baal's titles.

The Ancient of Days enthrones this one who appears human but is divine and gives him dominion over all the nations and people of the world. All authority that belonged for a time to the beasts is given to him, and his kingdom and reign extend into eternity (v. 14). The fulfillment in the New Testament is clear: Christ's Ascension into heaven describes Him as being seated on a cloud, connecting that event to Daniel's vision (e.g., Acts 1:9). The Ascension is the celebration not of Christ's "going away" but rather of his enthronement at the right hand of the Father.

An audience familiar with the Baal Cycle would recognize something else about this prophetic vision: They would notice that the description of the Ancient of Days sounds a lot like the iconography of El, Baal's father. They would notice the Baal language regarding "the one like a Son of Man." They also would recognize from the Baal Cycle the action of the scene in the enthronement of Baal within his palace, as this event was celebrated annually and at the dedication of one of Baal's temples. Here, however, the imagery has been remixed.

The figure of Baal, in Daniel's version, is this final and terrible beast—an ancient, dreadful, fallen angelic being who is put down and imprisoned in the underworld. Meanwhile, in the place of a supposedly victorious Baal is this human—this Son of Man, the seed of a woman—who is being enthroned instead. Here, an obedient and faithful Son, the express image of His Father, is the one who is given dominion, not Baal. The reason for this enthronement is, in part, that He has defeated Baal and freed the nations from his corruption.

The connection here is carried within Holy Tradition through the second major liturgical use of Psalm 24/23. In addition to its usage as a description of the Harrowing of Hades by Christ at Pascha, this text also is used in the liturgical hymns of Christ's Ascension. Christ is enthroned not in Baal's palace in the underworld but in the heavenly places. Here again, the cry of "Lift up your heads, O ye gates" is used as a taunt directed at the claims of Baal's supposed victory in some sort of revolution. The text is also used in some traditions at the dedication of a new church building—a new temple in which Christ will be enthroned, more glorious than the "palace" of the fallen Baal.

Finally, this contrast between the figure of Baal as the disobedient son of God and Christ as the true Son of God appears in the iconography and liturgical texts associated with the Baptism of Christ at the feast of Holy Theophany. In the icon, Christ is trampling serpents underfoot and driving the figures of Yam and Nahar (Sea and River) out of the Jordan River, both defeating the serpent and being the true victor over primordial chaos—a title that Baal seeks to claim. The readings for the great blessing of the waters include the defeat of Baal at Mount Carmel through Elijah. The prayers bluntly state that Christ has crushed the power of Baal.

Through a variety of genres of literature in texts written over the course of the better part of a millennium, the Old Testament describes a fallen divine being, a rebellious angelic figure, who was cast out of the realm of God and into the underworld. This demonic being, who would come to be known as the Devil, is identified with Baal. This is the same demonic Baal who has, with his lies and his false gospel, ensnared the nations through false worship, idolatry, and sexual immorality. In disrupting his lies, the Old Testament begins to lay out the blueprint of the truth that will come to fruition in the New Testament.

CHAPTER FOUR

Baal Bonds

What Happens to Baal in the New Testament?

B Y THE FIRST CENTURY AD, worship of Baal was of far less prominence in the ancient world. The cult persisted well into the third century, but the Roman world brought other cults, from both west and east, to the Levant and Syria. Integration of various groups into the wider Roman culture likewise drew significantly more popularity and attention to these religious practices over against those of their local ancestors. The older traditional forms were preserved primarily among native Syrians, most of them non-Roman citizens who still spoke Aramaic and later Syriac.

Much of what we know about the late stage of the Baal cult comes through Berossus, a priest of Baal living in Mesopotamia, who had been assimilated with the worship of Marduk.[1] Berossus was aware that he was a preserver of ancient, now mostly vanished traditions and sought to record them in the Greek language. His works have not

---

1   Marduk was being worshiped by this time as Bel-Marduk. *Berossus* is likely a
     Greek transliteration of the Akkadian for "Baal is his shepherd."

survived to the present day, but discussions of his work and its contents, as well as certain quotations, have been preserved in the works of others. His literary corpus includes not only religious matters but also records of Babylonian history and other cultural traditions.

Because of the waning of Baal worship, the New Testament interacts with Baal traditions in a very different way from the Old. The New Testament writers operate in a thought world formed by the Hebrew Scriptures. They think of the world in ways shaped by the Old Testament, including its use of the figure of Baal. The later assimilation of the figure of Baal to Zeus and Jupiter likewise creates a fusion of those traditions in the writings of the New Testament. The Old Testament's critique of Baal worship becomes a critique in the New Testament of the worship of Zeus and Jupiter, and thereby the entire Roman cult. Passages from the Hebrew Bible rework the contest between Baal and Mot as the eventual triumph of Yahweh over the powers of death and Sheol, and this material becomes a framework for expressing the gospel of Jesus Christ.

Beelzebub

BY THE TIME OF THE writing of the New Testament, the interpretation of the texts described in the previous chapter, as well as others, coalesced around the idea of a paradigmatic divine rebel who had been cast from heaven into the underworld by the true God. A variety of names and titles were used for this rebel in the literature of the Second Temple period, but the figure of Baal formed the contours of this being. Baal as a successful revolutionary was replaced by the Hebrew Scriptures' depiction of his failure. Nevertheless, this failed being became, through his temptation of humanity, the author of sin and destruction in the world who led humans to death.

Before discussing several of the biblical names for this figure, it is worth noting that his existence was so broadly accepted that he often didn't need to be named. In many cases, in both the texts that make up the New Testament and in other extra-biblical texts, he is simply called "the evil one." Additionally, a number of different strands of tradition emerged over the centuries following the Babylonian Exile of Judah. In general, the name given to this being in a text reveals and explains where that text is located within Jewish tradition.

This sorting is even evident in the books of the New Testament. Certain books and certain authors tend to favor particular names. For example, "the evil one" or "the wicked one" appears most commonly in texts written by St. John and St. Matthew (Matt. 13:19, 38; John 17:15; 1 John 2:13–14; 3:12; 5:18–19). Saint Paul also uses the term, but within his writings, he uses a variety of names and titles for this being. Some of them, like Belial, are unique among New Testament authors (Eph. 6:16; 2 Thess. 3:3). These terms reveal that St. Paul was conversant with a number of disparate strands of Jewish tradition.

The most prominent use of the title "the evil one" may be the Lord's Prayer as recorded in St. Matthew's Gospel (Matt. 6:13). The Greek here, however, is ambiguous as to whether the one praying is asking for deliverance from evil itself or the evil one as an agent. This equivocation may be deliberate, as it was common in Hebrew and Aramaic to use an ambiguous form of a word in order to imply several possible meanings at the same time.

Some of the names given to this evil spiritual being betray the direct connection to the figure of Baal. The most obvious of these is Beelzebub, sometimes rendered in New Testament manuscripts Beelzebul, which actually is the more accurate transliteration. *Beelzebul* is a Greek transliteration of an Aramaic title for Baal that means roughly "Baal is lord" or "the great lord Baal."[2] But as was common, Jewish people who did not want to make such a declaration replaced that title with a parody. *Beelzebub* means, literally, "lord of the flies."

---

2   It is the masculine form of the likely given name of Jezebel.

Based on Baal's association with death and the underworld, this may be a reference to a rotting carcass where flies congregate. And given Baal's connections to the bull and fertility, this may also be a reference to animal excrement, where flies do likewise.

This name, identifying the evil one as Baal, is used in the synoptic Gospels. Beelzebub is referred to in what appears to be three accounts of the same event (Matt. 12:24–27; Mark 3:22; Luke 11:14–19). Certain members of the party of the Pharisees, upon witnessing Jesus performing miracles in general and casting out demons in particular, accuse Him of doing so by the power of Beelzebub. Christ points out that this is a ridiculous suggestion, that a demon would cast out other demons. Matthew also uses "Beelzebub" elsewhere in an apparent reference to this exchange (Matt. 10:25).

Importantly, however, the Gospel accounts identify Baal here as the prince of demons. As in the Baal Cycle, Baal was a rebel against the Most High God, but he also recruited other spiritual beings to join in his rebellion. He is not a singular figure, an anti-God or an evil god. He is merely the prime example and the first of spiritual beings who rebelled against God in the way that Cain was depicted in Jewish literature as the archetypal sinner. There were many others like Baal who took the same path of destruction, and other lines of tradition will connect the fall of this primary rebellious spirit to the fall of the others.

Within the diverse Jewish traditions of the first century, there was one central belief regarding the origin of the other demonic spirits in the world. This story is told in the Book of Enoch (or 1 Enoch) and Jubilees and is referenced throughout the literature of the time, including the New Testament. Here, the first rebel is identified as Azazel, the author of sin and evil associated with the Day of Atonement ritual (Lev. 16). Azazel leads a group of angelic beings in rebellion against God. That rebellion produces a group of mortal "sons" of these demonic powers through engaging in rituals that involve human sacrifice, cannibalism, and sexual immorality. Aza-zel's co-rebels are imprisoned in the deepest part of the underworld. Their children, designated Nephilim, or "giants," are destroyed in the Flood in the days of Noah. The spirits of some of the Nephilim still wander the earth as demonic spirits.

BAAL AS SATAN AND THE DEVIL

THE TWO MOST COMMON NAMES for the divine rebel figure in the New Testament and throughout later Christian Tradition are Satan and the Devil. The title *Satan* is a transliteration of the Hebrew word meaning "adversary" or "opponent." Meanwhile, *Devil* is a transliteration of the Greek word *diabolos*, which refers to a "slanderer" or a "betrayer." In general, the Greek term is used as a translation for the Hebrew term and refers to the same spiritual being. Both these names are descriptors, meaning that there are many more slanderers than just the Devil, and there are many more adversaries than Satan. Nevertheless, when used as a title, these terms indicate that this angelic rebel is The Slanderer and The Adversary writ large.

Scholars of the history of religion make much of the fact that the figure in the Book of Job, referred to there as "the Satan," does not correspond to certain later ideas in the Christian Tradition of Satan or the Devil. This argument is, for the most part, overblown. The figure in Job is performing a particular function within the council of God—that of the accuser of the righteous. His playing of this role is seen as being incompatible with the idea that he is a rebel who has been cast out, and his role in the divine economy is even taken to mean that he can't be evil.

This view betrays a startling lack of understanding of the Hebrew Scriptures, in which everything—including evil itself—is understood to play a part in the divine economy. God is depicted as controlling the demonic forces of famine, violence, and plague, giving them leash as needed to render judgment and bring people to repentance. Why would a fallen angelic rebel be any different? This understanding of judgment was, in the first century, the general Jewish understanding of why God allowed demonic spiritual forces to operate in the world.

The spiritual being in Job, identified as one of the "sons of God" à la Baal, is playing a particular role for as long as God allows it: to accuse the righteous of their sin. This role is in keeping with the general role attributed to the fallen rebel elsewhere in Scripture. As the lord and eater of the dead, he lays claim to the dead based on their sin. Once Christ makes atonement for sin, he no longer has this power and is cast out of this role (Luke 10:18). He loses the ability to claim the righteous and thereby loses the power of death (Heb. 2:14).

Before the work of Christ, the whole world outside of Israel, and to some extent Israel itself as well, was under this power of death due to sin. In Israel, through the Torah, sin was managed and controlled. The rule of sin gave the Devil a certain kind of rulership over the world in that age. Scripture refers to his rulership several times, though always as something that was brief and is now coming to an end (John 12:31; 14:30; 16:11; 2 Cor. 4:4; 1 John 5:19). This power allowed the Devil to offer Christ all the kingdoms of the world if He would worship him (Matt. 4:7–9; Luke 4:5–7).

The Devil, Zeus

THE UNDERSTANDING THAT BAAL, BY various names, had come to rule the world was not only a theological matter but a political one in the first century AD. Alexander the Great had begun the process of reassimilating Zeus and Baal four centuries earlier. In Judea, the returning exiles of Judah had found themselves under the domination first of the Seleucid Greeks and then the Roman Empire. The Greeks, of course, regarded Zeus as the highest god, the father of gods and men. He was the first Panhellenic god and served as a culturally unifying force.

Unifying with Syrian and Phoenician culture through the identification of Zeus with Baal had worked well in large swathes of the newly emerging Greek world. However, attempts to make some form of Zeus as the god of Judea and Samaria had not gone as well. While the Persians had broadly tolerated the peculiarities of Jewish practices, the Greeks were less generous. They used the Judeans as a scapegoat for military defeats and natural disasters. Clearly, it was their refusal to worship the gods in general, and Zeus in particular, that had brought about these crises.

The sine qua non such incident happened under Antiochus IV Epiphanes in 167 BC. After losing a battle against the Ptolemaic ruler of Egypt, Antiochus blamed the Judeans' and Samaritans' lack of worship directed toward Zeus. He then moved in and rededicated the temples in both Jerusalem and Mount Gerizim to the worship of Zeus, offering pigs as sacrifices on the altars. According to Jewish sources, the Samaritans largely accepted that the "great god" whom they had been worshiping was the newly named "Zeus Hellenios" or "Zeus of the Greeks." But many Judeans referred to him instead as *Xenios*, or "he of the foreigners."

The desecration of the Jewish temple, referred to as "the abomination that brings desolation" in the Book of Daniel (9:27; 11:31), triggered a broad Jewish revolt against Greek imperial rule. The word translated as "bringing desolation" in Hebrew is *meshomem*, which is likely a play on the title *Baalshamin*, an Aramaic name for Zeus based on one of Baal's titles, "lord of the heavens." The Maccabee brothers led the revolt and took vengeance for the many Jewish people who had been martyred by the Greeks for refusing to participate in pagan worship or otherwise violate the commandments of the Torah.

This revolt produced an independent Judea ruled by the Hasmonean dynasty for a little over a century. To cement her independence from the Seleucids, however, the Hasmoneans put Judea into treaty arrangements with Sparta and Rome. Later, in the imperial period, Rome used these agreements as a pretext for the annexation of Judea and the oppression of the Jewish people. The Roman approach to Judea was less overtly hostile than the Greeks', though the same cannot be said in the other direction. Significant parties within Judea held the Maccabean martyrs and warriors in high esteem and sought to overthrow Roman rule. The Roman response to this was, over the course of a century, to turn from general tolerance of Jewish practice to an attempt to wipe out the Jewish presence in Judea completely.

The Roman Jupiter was known to be a more Western adaptation of the same traditions that produced the figure of Zeus. The name is likely derived from the Greek *Iopater,* regarded as the father of all (Greek) people. The name of Noah's son Japeth is an incorporation of this name into the Book of Genesis, where he is presented as the father of the peoples of Asia Minor and Greece. Worship of an ancestral father and king merged with storm-god traditions, received from Syria and Indo-European sky-god traditions, to produce the figure of Jupiter, who also rebelled against his father and ascended to become king of the gods.

Jupiter was clearly Zeus, and Zeus was, both to Jewish people of the first century and the other residents of Judea and neighboring provinces, clearly Baal. Through the Roman Empire, he had come to exert a malign power over the world, and most of the peoples worshiped him rather than the true God. This idea was so taken for granted that it allows for casual offhand references in the literature of the period. For example, in the letter to Pergamon in the Book of Revelation, St. John can refer to the high altar of the victory of Zeus there as "the throne of Satan" (Rev. 2:13).

This identification affected the general hope of the Jewish people. This hope, as defined from the Torah onward, had always been that the day would come when Yahweh the God of Israel would intervene in the history of the world to deliver His people from their enemies. For the Old Testament prophets, this deliverance included the promise of justice—that the kings of the nations who oppressed Israel would face the same fate that had befallen the spiritual rebel whom they worshiped and followed. This being had bedeviled and deceived all the nations, subjecting them all to Rome, so spiritual warfare and political liberation were bound together. The promised Messianic king of the line of David would need not only to reestablish the kingdom of Israel, He would need to judge the Devil once and for all and put him in his place.

The Antichrist

ONE TITLE FOR THE EVIL one that has not yet been discussed is *Belial*. The verbal connection between Belial and Baal, particularly Bel, as he was known in Babylonian rites, is obvious. Though there is some debate as to the origin of this form of the name, scholars generally consider it to be derived from the Aramaic *Beli ol*, or "yokeless one." Here, "yoke" is a reference to the Torah; to be yokeless is to be lawless. The Ascension of Isaiah, an extra-biblical text of the same period as the New Testament, refers to Belial as "the angel of lawlessness who is the ruler of this world" (*Asc. Isa.* 2:4). Saint Paul contrasts this name in 2 Corinthians 6:15 with the name of Christ.

In Jewish literature of the Second Temple period, the idea that the coming Messiah would engage in a showdown with Belial to usher in the Messianic Age is nearly ubiquitous. The people, even the kings, of the pagan nations are referred to as the "sons of Belial." A son is the image of his father; thus the political and material forces arrayed against God's people are deceived, empowered, and motivated by this dark spiritual being that stands behind them.

In the Hebrew prophets, the theme of judgment coming upon the nations for their wickedness is paired with the competing theme that these nations, in whole or in part, will eventually come to worship the God of Israel. The prophets reconciled this dissonance by seeing the victory of God and His Messiah in spiritual terms. Spiritual warfare is the true warfare. Once Belial is defeated, his orphaned sons can be adopted by a true Father. The defeat of the Devil is the reconciliation and healing of the nations from the sin into which he deceived them (Rev. 12:9; 22:2).

The coming Messiah was seen as the Son of God in a variety of senses. The term "sons of God," as we have seen, was applied to particular angelic beings, including the Devil before his fall. Even before the Birth of Jesus of Nazareth and the beginnings of nascent Christianity, Jewish literature began, based on this usage, to posit that the Messiah was, in some sense, a preexistent divine figure who was the true and perfect Image of God, over against the false and rebellious "son." These ideas were fulfilled—and filled to overflowing—in the reality of the Incarnation of Christ.

Humans were also, in some circumstances, identified as the sons of God. God's people Israel looked to Him as a father. Within this broader application, however, the king of Israel and later of Judah was seen as the son of the God of Israel in a unique sense, in serving as His image on earth. Psalm 2:7–8 was used as part of the coronation of a king in Judah.[3] The Messiah then, as the fulfillment of the Davidic line, would also be the fulfillment of this divine Sonship. The voice of the Father speaks these verses at Jesus' Baptism at the hand of St. John the Forerunner to confirm His Messianic identity.

As history progressed, the Baal-worshiping nations around Israel, Judah, and Judea coalesced into a series of empires. These empires,

---

3   "Yahweh said to me, 'You are my son, today I have begotten you. Ask me, and I will give you the nations for your inheritance and the far reaches of the world as your kingdom.'"

under one name or another, worshiped and served the same figure known as Baal. At the top of these empires was a single man who claimed to rule the world. This man also claimed to be a god and took for himself titles that rightly belonged only to the true God who created the world. Each of these particular sons of Belial, each of these kings, began to be seen as an anti-Messiah. He was the representative of that dark power on earth and wielded the Devil's power and authority, generally against the people of God. Texts during this period begin to portray the final battle or contest between the Messiah and Belial as one between the Messiah and Belial's representative on earth.

This identification was greatly aided by the propaganda issued by the Roman Empire about its emperors, beginning with Augustus. The Roman emperor claimed to be the son of a god—divine himself, the savior of the world, the lord of all the earth, and the father of all men. In addition to reigning as emperor and commanding the largest and most powerful army in the history of the world to date, he was the *pontifex maximus*, the high priest of the Roman religion, offering sacrifices to Jupiter and the other gods.

By the time of the composition of the texts that became the New Testament, the idea of this anti-Messiah, or, in Greek, *Antichrist*, was well known. New Testament authors can refer to it in passing. Saint John can say, "You have been told that an antichrist is coming" without the need for further explanation (1 John 2:18; 4:3). Saint Paul can speak to the Thessalonian Christians about the "man of lawlessness" or "man of Belial" who will be revealed (2 Thess. 2:3–10). Paul shorthands several aspects of this tradition, speaking of this figure setting himself up as a king and a god, working wonders by the energies of Satan, and being destroyed by the wrath of Jesus when He appears. Saint John, in the Book of Revelation, is even more on the nose in his description, using the Roman emperor Nero as an example of the type (Rev. 13:1–18).

For Christians as much as any other Jewish group, Rome was the manifestation of the rule of Satan over their present evil age. The Christian gospel, the proclamation of Jesus of Nazareth as the Christ, the Messiah who had conquered the Devil worshiped by Rome and taken his power, challenged Rome's gospel just as much as it had challenged the Baal Cycle in centuries past. Those false gospels were, for Christians, all one deception.

Unlike many other Jewish groups, however, and following the lead of St. Paul, the Christian approach to countering this deception was not based in military efforts patterned after the Hasmoneans. Early Christianity understood that the real warfare was spiritual warfare. The cure for the deception of the Devil was the truth of the gospel of Christ. This was true not only for the regular people of the nations who had been subjected to Rome and also subjected to the demonic powers by false, pagan worship, this was true all the way up to the emperor, the Antichrist himself, whom St. Paul sought not to defeat or kill but to convert. When that great representative of the power of Baal on earth converted to Christianity in the reign of St. Constantine, the entire world was transformed.

Skip Baal

Why Is Baal Still Important?

M ODERN SOCIETY LOVES A REBEL. No one makes movies about cops who play by the rules. Possibly the most popular fantasy franchise of the last fifty years, *Star Wars*, focuses on a heroic "rebel alliance" battling an evil empire. Flowing from the writing of Milton and the art of William Blake, the Devil himself became a romantic figure. The author Albert Camus wrote extensively on this idea of rebellion and the pursuit of freedom. Specifically, he described how that rebellious impulse ends in self-destruction.

Real freedom is the freedom to do good. It is freedom to grow and flourish. While evildoing, the example of the Devil, always offers the promise of freedom, it delivers only slavery to sin and ultimate death. To be truly free is not to be able to choose to do whatever one wants in the hope of avoiding the consequences of choices. To be free is not to rule one's self, to be under no authority, to forge one's own path that leads to Hades. Instead, one finds freedom in coming under the good and righteous authority of God and by walking a path not only already laid out but already trod by Christ and His saints.

Those who in the ancient world worshiped Baal—the Canaan-ites, the Phoenicians, and others—were told a story. It was a story of rebellion, of conquest, of freedom from everything—even, poten-tially, death. They not only heard this story told, they participated in it through dark rites that now offend us morally. Worse than this moral offense, though, is the fact that the story is a lie. The story leads those who live it to the netherworld, indeed, but not as free people. The story leads its followers to destruction.

The Scriptures correct this story. They tell the truth of where a rebel like Baal ended up. They tell the truth about where he is leading his worshipers and followers. Baal's false story is a false gospel. It tells of victories that were, in fact, defeats. It praises someone unworthy of praise for deeds left undone. It steals for Baal claims of glory and power that rightly belong to the true God. This story is a weapon of the evil one who brought whole nations to share in his fate. This story encouraged them to commit atrocities.

More important than correcting the record, the Scriptures tell another story. They tell a true story of the true Son of God, the Lord Jesus the Messiah. They tell the story of His real victories, culminat-ing in His victory over death. This true gospel, this true story, is also one that the followers of Christ participate in through ritual. But it is a story that leads His followers to the end of Christ's journey—to resur-rection, glorification, and eternal life. The telling of this story, partici-pating in it, and living it out in one's own life, is the core of Christianity.

Understanding Baal's false story, its pernicious twisting of the truth that was found so attractive and powerful to so many in the ancient world, helps bring the truth of Christ's story into sharper relief. As always, the Devil is a parasite. He cannot create; he can only twist and distort. But this means that all his efforts to spread his lies ultimately also spread the framework for the Truth—a framework that aids the benighted followers of Baal and his ilk to better under-stand the reality of Christ when He is presented to them.

This is an answer to the question, "Why?" Why would God allow these lies to be told? Why would He allow entire generations to follow the Devil's path to destruction? Why would He allow the Devil to be active at all? Because God is able to bring, and concretely has brought, good and truth out of the Devil's lies and their exposure. By allowing humans to choose slavery and death, He gives them an understanding of what it means to be free and to live. By allowing the propagation of the story of a false and rebellious son of God, He prepared the way for His true, faithful, and righteous Son to come and destroy the works of the Devil.

Subject Index

We hope you have enjoyed and benefited from this book. Your financial support makes it possible to continue our nonprofit ministry both in print and online. Because the proceeds from our book sales only partially cover the costs of operating **Ancient Faith Publishing** and **Ancient Faith Radio**, we greatly appreciate the generosity of our readers and listeners. Donations are tax deductible and can be made at **www.ancientfaith.com.**

To view our other publications,
please visit our website: **store.ancientfaith.com**

ANCIENT FAITH
RADIO

Bringing you Orthodox Christian music, readings, prayers, teaching, and podcasts 24 hours a day since 2004 at
www.ancientfaith.com